A People Without a Country:
Country:
Voices from Palestine

A People Without a Country:
Voices from Palestine

Marian Saadeh and Harry Katz, editors

authorHOUSE®

AuthorHouse™
1663 Liberty Drive
Bloomington, IN 47403
www.authorhouse.com
Phone: 1-800-839-8640

First published by AuthorHouse   08/09/2011

ISBN: 978-1-4634-4756-4 (sc)
ISBN: 978-1-4634-4755-7 (ebk)

Library of Congress Control Number: 2011914156

Printed in the United States of America

Contents

Introduction

The intention of this compilation of essays, stories, poems, and illustrations, *A People Without a Country: Voices from Palestine,* is to provide the reader with simple and honest accounts of the kinds of experiences Palestinians-particularly younger people—have had under Israeli occupation. Most Americans-such as myself—have had absolutely no exposure to the world of Palestinians;everything we know is filtered through the media or what we are programmed to believe.

I had become interested in the plight of Palestinians when it began to dawn on me that they were the victims of injustice, that they were being displaced and pushed out of-or squeezed into—lands that had been in their families and communities for centuries, and that they had begun to lose the right to move around freely, among other things. It had begun to disturb me that most people I knew, politicians, and the media had no knowledge of their plight, and worse, were indifferent to what was, most definitely, oppression and persecution. Once a strong supporter of Israel, I now perceived that country as an occupying power that trampled upon the local

Palestinian citizenry, and expected the world to look the other way when it engaged in all sorts of intimidating and ruthless actions, many of which will come to light in this compilation.

The disappointment I felt in Israel as a Jew, and the outrage as a human being, compelled me to take action. First I made modest donations to Bethlehem University, a Catholic University under the La Salle order that has served Palestinian youth since 1973, and then with the help of Brother Jack Curran, Vice President for Development at BU, I made contact with Marian Saadeh, who had just graduated from the University with a degree in Psychology. She agreed to go in with me on a project to bring the voices of Palestinian youth to the United States and other English speaking countries. Over a period of a half year she solicited, compiled, translated, and edited many articles and poems from everyday people about life in the Holy Lands—as Palestinians refer to their area. I was deeply moved by the powerful and unaffected simplicity of these pieces.

Marian is a Christian Palestinian, a group of people who are rapidly disappearing in the Holy Land, the birthplace of Jesus. Palestinian Christians now make up less than 4% of the Palestinian population of which they were a majority, in places like Bethlehem, at the time of the rebirth of Israel. It is clear to me that the unreasonable policies of Israel have contributed to the slow cultural and demographic genocide of these people. Her family has been living in Bethlehem for many generations and her father, who was trained as an engineer in the U.S., came back to the Holy Land in the 1980's to work as the headmaster of a Christian school and to serve as a Deputy Mayor of Bethlehem. I was saddened, beyond words to learn, early on in our correspondence, of the death of Marian's sister, Christina, at age nine, by the Israeli Defense Force in a mistaken identity drive-by shooting.

Both Christian and Moslem Palestinians contributed to this book, which I edited only to correct major grammatical errors. I did not edit content—emotional or factual.

It's quite hard for me to accept the reality that I, as a Jewish American, can take up residence in Israel and become a citizen of that nation, although there are no known relatives of mine in that country, and none as far back as our family's genealogical records go, while a Palestinian living in Bethlehem,

Gaza, or any of the occupied territories whose family has been there for centuries has no country to call his or her own, and is a legal citizen of no land. To say nothing of the millions of Palestinians driven out or expelled from the Holy Land during Israel's war for independence and the wars that followed. The re-creation of Israel, contrary to what I was taught throughout my childhood, was not just a simple victory for one group of people, but a tragedy beyond words for another group, the effects of which are still reverberating throughout the world.

Another factor that personally contributed to my interest in the Palestinians and their cause is the simple fact that our son is of Palestinian ancestry(in that his maternal grandfather was born in Bethlehem) as well as Jewish, a Jewish Palestinian. Indeed, his roots, both Biblical and genealogical, are in the Holy Land.

I hope that this book will convey a sense of what life is like for Palestinians living under Israeli occupation, and that, somehow, it will contribute not only to a better understanding between Palestinians and Jews, but to peace.

Harry Katz

A Brief History of Palestine

Sixty-two years after the catastrophe of 1948, forty-three years after the occupation of the West Bank, East Jerusalem and the Gaza Strip, the Palestinian people are still struggling to give credibility, believability and responsibility to a very unconvincing peace process. The Palestinians are still suffering from three successive denials: their mere physical existence, their basic human rights, and finally the recognition of our suffering which was constantly trivialized. The development of a modern Palestinian identity and expression of self-determination has focused upon the recent rather than the ancient past. Palestinian history is concerned only with the last couple of centuries in the struggle with the Zionist movement and the realization of a modern state of Israel. The ancient past belongs to Israel since this is the way it has been presented from the inception of modern biblical studies. It is as if the ancient past has been abandoned to Israel.

Edward Said's "Blaming the Victims" opens with the observation that Palestine has been the home to a remarkable civilization, centuries before the first Hebrew tribes migrated to the area. The people of Palestine have lived there forever, since time immemorial. They are the original inhabitants and occupants of this territory. They have always been in possession of their land.

The aim of this essay, therefore, is to briefly describe Palestine History within this frame.

Palestine's location at the center of routes linking the three continents made it a meeting place for religious and cultural influences from Egypt, Syria, Mesopotamia and Asia Minor. In addition, it was the natural battleground for the great powers of the region and subject to dominations by adjacent empires.

In the third millennium B.C, the Canaanites were the earliest known inhabitants of Palestine (Semitic tribes from the Arab Peninsula). The second millennium B.C saw Egyptian hegemony and Canaanite autonomy which were constantly challenged by ethnically diverse invaders, such as the Amorites, Hittites, and Hurrians who were defeated by the Egyptians and absorbed by the Canaanites.

In the 14th century B.C, new invaders appeared, the Hebrews, a group of Semitic tribes from Mesopotamia and the Philistines, (after whom the country was later named) an Aegean people.

In 1230 B.C, Joshua conquered parts of Palestine and settled in the hill country.

In 1125 B.C, the Israelites (a confederation of Hebrew tribes) defeated the Canaanites but struggles continued with the Philistines.

The first Millennium B.C saw the emergence of David, the King of Israel who established a large independent state, followed by his son Solomon. After his death the kingdom was divided into Israel in the North and Judah in the South.

Between 722-721 B.C, Israel fell to Assyria, and in 586 B.C Judah was conquered by Babylonia, who destroyed Jerusalem and exiled most of the Jews while the temple was sacked.

In 539, Persia conquered Babylonia and permitted Jews to return to Judea. In the year 333 B.C, Greece ruled the country by Alexander the Great of Macedonia, followed by the Ptolemis of Egypt and the Seleucids of Syria (who tried to impose Hellenistic culture and religious on the population).

In 63 B.C, Jerusalem was overrun by Rome. Herod was appointed king of Judea and extended and restored the second Temple. During his rule Jesus of Nazareth began his teaching mission and later was tried and sentenced to death. Emperor Titus laid siege to Jerusalem, destroyed the Herodian temple, and built the new city, Aelia.

In 313 A.D, Roman Emperor Constantine legalized Christianity and his mother, Helena, built the Church of the Nativity, and the Church of the Holy Sepulcher.

Roman rule was interrupted, however, by a brief Persian occupation and ended when the Muslim Arab Armies invaded Palestine in 638. Its boundaries, its characteristics including its name in Arabic, Filastine, became known to the entire Islamic world as much as its fertility, and its beauty as for its religious significance.

George Sandys, the English poet, spoke of Palestine as a land that flowed with milk and honey. During the Umayyad caliphate the importance of Palestine as a holy place for Muslims was emphasized.

In 750, Palestine passed to the Abbasid caliphate, and their period was marked by unrest. In the 9th century, Palestine was conquered by the Fatimides dynasty and Palestine became a battlefield (996-1021). Christians and Jews were suppressed and many churches were destroyed.

In 1090, Palestine was captured by the Crusaders, who established the Latin Kingdom. Jews, Muslims as well as Orthodox Christians were seen as infidels and were slaughtered in and around Jerusalem.

In 1187, the Crusaders were defeated by Saladin at the battle of Hittin.

Mongol invaders from East Asia destroyed many villages but were defeated by the Egyptian Mamluks, who ruled Palestine from 1250 to 1515.

The Administrative system during Mamluks' period was more organized and developed. Most of the lands were military fiefs. The Mamluks were the first who introduced the military feudal system in Palestine. They paid great attention to cultivate and develop the agricultural lands. Villagers paid their taxes from the proceeds of their harvests. At the end of the Mamluks' period, Palestine was in disarray . . . Heavy taxes were imposed on the population, divisions and quarrels between the Mamluks and princes increased, in addition to the spread of diseases, such as the Black Death, villages and towns were destroyed.

Two strong earthquakes in 1458 and 1497 t were followed by severe drought, which was considered the worst period in the history of Palestine.

1517-1915: the Ottomans defeated the Mamluks in 1516, and their rule spread all over the Middle Eastern countries. Palestine was divided into several districts (sanjaks). Christians and Jewish communities were allowed a large measure of autonomy.

The first three centuries of the Ottoman rule isolated Palestine from outside influence and the country.

Under the Ottomans, the Arabs formed an important part of the structure of the Ottoman Empire. The head of the administration was the Vali in Beirut. Jerusalem was an independent Sanjak (district); the remainder of Palestine was included in the Willayat (governorate) of Beirut, Acre, and Balko. Each Sanjak was divided into Qadas (districts) combining several Nahiyas (combined villages). Each had its own council and posse of executive officials. This administrative structure was in effect during the Tanzimat (Reform) period in the 19th century.

Napoleon Bonaparte invaded Egypt in 1797 and advanced to Palestine but was defeated after he laid siege to Acre. His arrival heralded the advent of the modern Middle East.

In 1831, Muhammad Ali, the Egyptian Viceroy nominally subject to the Ottoman Sultan occupied Palestine. Under his rule and his son Ibrahim Basha, Palestine was opened to European influence. The Ottoman dynasty reasserted its rule in 1840.

During Ottoman rule the population of Palestine all spoke Arabic, and were mainly Sunni Muslims, although a minority among them were Christian. Approximately 65% of the Palestinian Arabs were agricultural people who lived in about 500 villages. There were also a respectable Palestinian, intellectual, and professional class, the beginning of small industries, and a highly developed national consciousness. The last quarter of the 19th century saw the determination of the Ottomans to impose their centralized policy of direct control. They launched a systematic military campaign to subjugate and break the power of local lords.

A new order was emerging with a new structure of administration, which linked the territory directly to Istanbul. The opening of the Suez Canal in 1869, and the building of the Hijaz railway and the invention of the telegraph made it possible for the Ottomans to extend their influence and directly control the country. Electoral law went into effect in 1876. Thousands of Palestinian Muslim soldiers were killed in the Russo-Turkish War of 1877-1878.

After 1908 Ottoman reforms in Palestine allowed people to express their opinion more freely. Several local newspapers were established in Jaffa, Jerusalem and Haifa. Europeans were active and were encouraged to visit Palestine. Most European states opened their consulates in Jerusalem.

After 1882, Jewish arrival in Palestine began. Various English statesmen gave political support to the idea of the establishment of a National home in Palestine for the Jewish people. Zionism was defined by Theodor Herzl, an Australian Jew, who in 1897 in the Congress of Jews stated: "it is the effort to win a legally-secured, publicly-recognized home for the Jewish people in Palestine".

On the outbreak of World War I (1914), Britain promised the independence of Arab lands and an end to Ottoman rule (including Palestine) in return for Arab support against Turkey, which had entered the war on the side of Germany.

In 1916, Britain and France signed the Sykes-Picot agreement, which divided the Arab countries into zones of influence. Palestine was occupied by the British.

On November 1917, the Earl of Balfour, at the time the Foreign Secretary of Britain made, on behalf of his majesty's government, the following historic Declaration:

"His majesty's government views with favor the establishment in Palestine of a National Home for the Jewish people, and will use their best endeavors to facilitate the achievement of that object."

The declaration was endorsed by the Allied Powers and embodied in the treaty of Sevres signed in 1920, whereby Turkey renounced her sovereignty over Palestine and authorized the country to be entrusted to a mandatory power to be approved by the League of Nations. Later, at San Remo-Italy in April 1920, the Mandate was entrusted to Great Britain. On the 24th of July 1922, the council of the League of Nations approved the Mandate of Palestine.

Palestinian Arabs opposed the Balfour Declaration and revolted against the migration of Jews to Palestine, which deepened Arab fears that the Zionist movement's aim was to establish a Jewish state in Palestine. In 1936, the Palestinians held a six month general strike to protest against the confiscation of land and Jewish immigration. In 1937, the Peel Commission headed by Lord Robert Peel issued the report in which the commission concluded that the mandate of Palestine was unworkable and recommended the partition of Palestine into a Jewish state and an Arab State.

In 1947, Great Britain decided to leave Palestine and called on the United Nations to convene and make recommendations. The UN convened on November 29, 1947 and adapted a plan calling for partition of Palestine into Jewish and Arab States with Jerusalem as an International zone under UN jurisdiction. Palestinians protested against the partition and revolted in violence. In 1948, the British withdrew on this day and war broke out between the Jewish and the Arabs supported by the armies of Egypt, Trans-Jordan, Syria, and Iraq. But the war failed to prevent the establishment of a Jewish state after UN arranged armistice agreements between Israel and Egypt, Lebanon, Jordan and Syria.

Here it is important to note that until the few weeks preceding the establishment of Israel, there was nothing other than a huge Arab majority. For example, the Jewish population in 1931 was 174,601 against a total of Arab Palestinians of 1,033,314 and in 1946, there were 608,225 Jews in a total population of 1,912,112.

In 1948, the population of Palestine was 74% Arab citizens and 26% Jewish citizens. Of more than 800,000 Arabs who lived in Israeli-held territory before 1948, only about 170,000 remained. The rest became refugees in the surrounding Arab countries, ending the Arab majority in the Jewish state.

In 1965 The Palestine Liberation Organization was established, and its main goal was the liberation of Palestine and the return of the Palestinian refugees who are scattered all over the Arab World.

In 1967 a war broke out between the Arab states of Egypt, Jordan, and Syria against Israel. The war ended with an Israeli victory and occupation of all the West Bank, Arab East Jerusalem, and the Gaza Strip. Several uprisings by the Palestinian broke out against the Israeli occupation, thousands were killed and imprisoned.

In 1973 Egypt and Syria attacked Israel, which was known as October War. The Egyptian forces crossed Suez channel, and Israel suffered a string of defeats, which were reversed, thanks to billions of dollars of military aid from the U.S. The Arab oil-producing states cut off petroleum exports to the United States and other Western nations in retaliation for their aid to Israel. Later, the USA sponsored a peace settlement between Israel and Egypt in Sinai, and between Israel and Syria in the Golan Heights in 1974.

In 1987 the Palestinians revolted and a series of uprising in the occupied territories that included demonstrations, strikes, and rock—throwing attacks on Israeli soldiers, which was known as the Intifada (uprise) of the Palestinian people.

In 1988 The Palestinian National Council meeting in Algiers declared the state of Palestine as outlined in the United Nation partition plan number 181.

In 1993 secret negotiations took place between the Palestinians and the Israelis during which Mr. Yitzak Rabin, Prime Minister of Israel, and PLO chairman, Mr. Yasser Arafat, signed a historic peace agreement, which was later called the Oslo Peace Agreement, whereby the Palestinians would have their own self rule for a temporary transitional period during which negotiation would take place to reach a final peace settlement.

Mr. Khalil Shokeh, A Palestinian Historian

A Hopeful Lament

Hopelessness beckons round every corner.
Lurking like a shadow, can't shake it off!
Despair and despondency creep into all parts of life,
each hour that passes, more pain and strife.
Enclosed by a wall made of concrete and steel
surrounded by barriers and checkpoints-
This birthplace of Jesus, now swamped by agony.
Violence and conflict, no peace, no calm.
Forgotten by the rest of the world,
No minds understand.
The pain and the hurting
The struggle for land.
How can I comprehend the promises of God?
When everything seems to go against Your great love.
What can I do but hold onto Your love?
Deliver us who trust, hold us firm in the storm.
So what breaks the hopelessness?
What calms the despair?
What takes away the pain?
What brings healing and repair?
Not the anger of man, or the pride of a sinner.
Not the wisdom of kings or international summits.
Through decades of anguish only one thing holds true,
The faithfulness and love of you, Christ.

Take all the evil and smash it as glass.
Grind it to nothing, then let your ways be a part-
of everything that moves, of everything you made,
In this we hold our hope, that one day Your ways prevail.

Grace Al-Zoughbi

All of a Sudden I found Myself in a New Place. What is it Going to be Like?

I never knew that I would get to that hospital or that I would meet all these people. I was afraid in the beginning and had lots of questions in my head like what will happen, where we are heading, who will meet us, and how will they treat us?

These questions only lasted for a while until we reached the hospital. We arrived by a private taxi owned by an Arab man from Jerusalem. My dad and I were heading to a hospital known as Hadassah, because my father was supposed to go through chemotherapy in the hospital for leukemia, also known as blood cancer.

When we reached the hospital, which was two sizes larger than the West Bank hospitals, we went into the reception. The Israeli flag was proudly displayed and I was a little scared since the room was full of people speaking Hebrew. Some of them were waiting their turn for treatment, some of them were accompanying patients, and the rest were staff at the hospital.

My dad talked to the receptionist and told her in Hebrew that his name was Fuad and that he was here to do the chemotherapy session we had arranged in advance. She looked at the papers and asked him to wait on the seats. We waited for a while until one of the staff, a nurse, came with a wheelchair and asked my father to sit in it. My father refused at first, but the nurse told him that these procedures are used for all patients, especially patients with cancer, so as to provide the best atmosphere for them.

We took the elevator to the second floor. My dad remained in the wheel chair and I followed him wherever he went. We entered another room, and the nurse asked us to wait a little bit until a bed was prepared for my dad's chemotherapy session. We didn't wait long before the nurse returned and asked us to move to the room that was prepared for my dad. Every time he spoke with my dad, the nurse called him *Mr. Fuad*, which caught my attention.

We moved into the room, which we shared with three other cancer patients. All of them were Jews who spoke no Arabic. They knew very well that we were Palestinians, however, and were there for the same reason: chemotherapy.

My father started talking to them in Hebrew, and I was constantly interrupting because I needed translation since I don't speak Hebrew. My father learned the language while he had worked in their areas, like all Palestinian workers who learned Hebrew to communicate with their coworkers. The patients talked mainly about the disease, but they also discussed the region in which we lived and other everyday things. I just sat there watching them.

When I looked at them I thought about the fear I felt on the way to the hospital because we were living in the West Bank under the occupation of the Israeli military. I also thought about how afraid I was that these people would treat us the way soldiers do at Israeli checkpoints, or the way Palestinians are treated when arrested or put in prison, but soon these concerns were alleviated.

What I thought of at that moment was how those patients, including my father, could overcome all the political issues and sit in the same room and share their lives' concerns without fighting over the land. I pondered how we could all gather in one six-square-meter room, and yet we were unable to live together in the same land. I felt like this thought itself could be a betrayal of my land and of the martyrs who were killed in Bethlehem that very day because of the occupation.

I didn't know if I could forgive myself for this kind of thinking, but then I remembered the humanity of the workers in the hospital and how they treated us with respect and care. All of a sudden I didn't know what was right or wrong anymore.

I decided to write this article because I can't hide this feeling anymore. Some might say that the way I talked about the staff of

Hadassah Hospital and their humanity is a kind of normalization, but I believe that the way they treated us was kindhearted, genuine, and based on their belief in their profession and commitment to help patients—no matter what their nationality. For them, everyone gets the same treatment.

Osamma Awaad

Bethlehem City

My name is Milad Hanna Azar, I'm a Palestinian guy who lives in Bethlehem, the city where Jesus Christ was born. I graduated from Bethlehem University, with a BS degree in Nursing and Health Sciences. I also used to be a member of Bethlehem University Student Ambassador Program (BUSAP) presenting Bethlehem University milestones to the visitors. Nowadays I'm working in a pediatric hospital at Bethlehem city.

Because of the shortage of nurses in the world, and the fact that I studied nursing it made it much easier for me to find a job than my friends. Those who graduated with a BS in Business or IT are still searching for jobs.

Traveling outside Palestine is a way they are hope to to find a job and continue their lives in safer place. The Israeli occupation of Palestinian territories plays a strong role in the situation facing the new Palestinian graduates as the whole Palestinian community at large.

Checkpoints, soldiers, weapons, and the Separating Wall are all reasons for the unsafe, dangerous and blockaded life. Peace is a project we are talking about but we have not been able to take a real step in that direction in our lives up to this point; we have been prevented from "walking the talk." Palestinians don't have freedom to move everywhere inside their country; they need permission to move from one side to the other side and if they don't get this permission they must stay in their district. Many children, tourists, and pilgrims know nothing about Palestine. Perhaps these school children studied about many places in Palestine but they have not been to these places; Tourism and pilgrims only go to the Israeli side where it is safe and where there are beautiful scenes. They don't see our daily suffering at the checkpoints, where time is worth nothing for the soldiers. Even in emergencies people could die waiting to get a piece of paper written on it that he can enter the Israeli territories—which is Palestinian land originally. History and archeology showed no evidence that Israel was here in the Past. But to talk to them about Palestine freedom makes you realize how similar it is to an imaginary task—with the absence of love and humility.

Talking about the health sector in Palestine makes you ask many questions with the low socioeconomic status, and the Palestinian—Israeli conflict. Simply put hospitals have very limited access to technology the way other countries do have, and you can't find good specialists among the doctors or the nurses. So when there are chronic or serious cases, the patients need to be transferred to near border countries to get good treatment and therapy. Otherwise limited treatment—at best—is available, due to low incomes and marginal hospitals.

I would like to end my essay with a prose poem written to Bethlehem City which shows how this city suffers from Israeli occupation of Palestinian territories, a place where peace should be, but darkness became the master.

Bethlehem My City

"Oh, my dear Bethlehem, what pain and suffering you are in. Where is the faith, love and peace that we used to have, feel and live in??"

"Ahhh, my dear friend, it is a long story that turns me from a charming star lit in the sky full of faith, to an ugly city full of darkness and death. War, my dear friend, destroys my ways to peace and justice. My enemies, dear friend, those who spread untruths, telling visitors that I'm a terrorist—people run terrified from me. They also pass near me looking without visiting . . . what a bad feeling, dear friend . . . I'm standing alone without any friends' support . . . In my heart, Jesus Christ, the Lord was born; the Virgin Mary was the first visitor written down in the history. Queen Helena was my first pilgrim . . . she ordered to build the oldest church in the world,

Nativity, in my lovely gardens, where also King David used to live. Oh, my dear friend, don't you see or hear what humans did to me?

They separate me from my other Palestinian cities, putting me in isolation like I have some contagious disease. My citizens used to light three candles inside my church for Peace, Love and Faith. When war turns off the first two, the faith candle is kept alight, holding the hope for peace in the near future. Each new lighted faith-candle asks God to give us a hand for peace. So, my dear friend, Bethlehem asks you for a prayer to have peace. It is the city where peace should be, but without justice, darkness became the master."

By: Milad Hanna Azar

Case Study

Clinical Picture:

Jad ElZughbi, 25 years old male living in Bethlehem-Jerusalem, single, BSC Occupational Therapy. Lives with his family, four brothers and one sister, father originally from Bethlehem, a city considered to be under the Palestinian Authority, and mother, originally from Jerusalem, which is considered under the Israeli authority.

To move from Bethlehem to Jerusalem a special permit is needed. During the last 27 years, his parents tried to get the Jerusalem ID for his father and the family (brothers and sister), and under different and difficult conditions, they got a paper with a temporary Jerusalem ID and ID numbers which were under special conditions, and that was good. When Jad turned 16, his brother and he got a scholarship to study in the USA; for that his brother applied for a travel document, and Jad applied for an ID (because under the law of Israel, the person has to be 16years old to get an ID). At that time, they didn't know that they were not allowed to travel while having the temporary ID, though they issued his brother the travel documents, and refused to issue him an ID. For no explanation, Jad remained without any documents (neither Israeli nor Palestinian) for 5 years.

Diagnosis:

The accused above-mentioned convicted of guilt and to live without any documents that prove identity. For five years, Jad tried to apply for a Jerusalemite ID, but he was rejected several times regardless of his efforts! He also applied to get a Palestinian ID, and finally got it after 5 years.

Treatment plan:

For a young man living in the Holy Land, without holding any documents that prove his identity, is illegal. Living in Jerusalem (the old city), is considered to be unsafe to move without an ID; wherever he wants to move or go, an ID is needed to prove identity, because the Israeli soldiers are everywhere, and they would stop anyone; for no reason they might humiliate and imprison anyone that they would suspect, so imagine they would stop a young guy and they wouldn't believe that he doesn't hold an ID, they would think that he is hiding something, and would bring him to jail:

- Imagine a 16 years old boy, living in the old city of Jerusalem, needs to go to his school which isn't far from his home (7 minutes walking) has to suffer daily from the fear that a soldier might stop him, and ask him for his ID, at least twice a day, once while going to school, and once while going back home.
- Imagine a 16 years old guy, who is not able to go out with his friends, can't visit his classmates, and can't go with them to a school trip. Once he asked his friend who went in a trip to Jabal ElShiek, to take pictures and to leave a place for him in the pictures so that he could feel as if here was with them in their trip.
- Imagine a guy in his own graduation from high school not being allowed to go to the party of his graduation because of the fear that he would be stopped by a police and asked to prove his identity.
- Imagine that this young man's father and uncles were not allowed to participate in his graduation because they were not able to get permission that allows them to go to Jerusalem.
- Imagine a guy that been given a high school certificate under his own name, but under an expired ID number.

- Imagine this same guy that been stopped by a gang, been roped and injured under threat, couldn't yell for police, help or even to go to a police station to complain and sue these guys.

After graduation Jad decided to continue his own studies, but what choices were available for him! A guy without any ID would not be able to study in any of the Israeli or Palestinian universities, for Not being able to register without an ID number, and Not being able to move from home to University. Already his choices for education are limited, but with his case, he has been directed to one choice: Bethlehem University. For it was the safest university, and for that there were people who could prove Jad's identity without the need of bringing ID number to register him, with the risk of not issuing a certification after graduation (for it won't be legal). Jad had to move to Bethlehem, in order to reduce the risk of being caught without an ID. In this situation Jad had to be separated from family members and live by himself in Bethlehem.

Jad thought that it would be easier to live in Bethlehem than Jerusalem, because he thought that being stopped by Israeli police would be less probable, but he was wrong, several times, Jad has to hide and take longer ways to get home, as a hunted person, so that he can avoid any police or soldiers. It could be worse to be stopped by Israeli soldiers in Bethlehem than in Israel, because they wouldn't differentiate between truth and fiction, and wouldn't listen to the real story. They would take anyone to the prison, without telling him to which prison and for how long, or why he is taken.

Jad thought that it would be easier to escape from the political situation, but it was hard for him to live away from his own family, and old friends. How many times he felt HOMESICK for not being able to see his family for weeks. He wasn't able to visit his own grandfather and grandmother, who were old and sick. Even when his grandfather died, he were not able to participate in the ceremony, or offer condolences to his grandmother. Jad was not able to participate in the his brothers' high school graduation; he was not able to celebrate Christmas Eve with his family, was not able to celebrate Easter days with his family, and was not able to celebrate his own birthday with his family.

Jad graduated with BSc degree in Occupational Therapy from Bethlehem University, but in order to graduate, he has to pass 1000 training hours in different organizations and associations, in different areas and cities. He tried with the cooperation of the university to complete as much as possible of these training hours in organizations and associations in the Bethlehem area, so as to avoid traveling to other cities, but that was not enough; there are not many organizations and associations in Bethlehem area that cover all the needed training hours; he needed to go to other cities. One of these organization was located in Al-Izarieh (a city to the east of Jerusalem), and to get there, Jad has to pass an Israeli checkpoint that separates one Palestinian city from another Palestinian city. It was a bit risky for Jad to pass it; 3 days a week, for two months, Jad had to pass through this checkpoint, with the risk that the soldiers might stop the car, and ask for IDs. Passing this checkpoint increased one thing in Jad's daily life; more prayers. Thanks to God, Jad passed this checkpoint several times without any problem or without being stopped, and as miracles do happen, even when they stopped the car and asked for some IDs the soldiers didn't ask for Jad's ID. Only once and in the last week of training, while Jad was going back from the training placement to Bethlehem, a political issue was raised and the checkpoint was too risky. For that Jad asked his supervisor to find him a place to sleep for that last week, so that he would not risk passing the checkpoint.

Another placement was located in Ramallah, and luckily this training happened to be for a total of 45 days without the need to go back for other courses in the university. For that Jad rented a room in Ramallah, and stayed there for these 45 days, completing his training, with the help of his colleagues who were going back and forth to Bethlehem on a daily basis, and brining him the reading materials that he needed—but of course it is never the same as doing it yourself. Also Jad was not able to see his other colleagues or family for these 45 days. But he was glad that he could achieve and complete these training hours. The only risk was twice, once while going to Ramallah, and the other time was going back to Bethlehem, for there were two checkpoints that separate the Palestinian cities from each other.

Prognosis, progress and regress:

Jad was a prisoner of his own world for 3 years in Bethlehem. During these three years Jad was trying so hard to get any ID, either a Jerusalemite ID, or a Palestinian ID, but he got none of them. Jad decided to give it a last try; he went to the internal office of Bethlehem, and asked to meet the director of the office. Forty five days later, Jad was volunteering in a summer camp, and in that day they were in a pool in Bethlehem, and Jad was supervising the kids while swimming, he got a call from the internal office telling him that a Palestinian ID has been issued to him. Unbelievably one good thing finally happened. This allowed him to, at least, be able to move in between the Palestinian cities without the great fear he had about being caught without an ID, "The funny thing is that when I started passing the checkpoints having my proof, I always wanted them to ask for my ID, so that I would show it up to them." It's much easier for him to move, but still finds it hard to live in Bethlehem away from his family who live in Jerusalem, and he needs a special permit to live with his family. Jad is out of "this prison," but under conditions & rules.

**Supervised and treated by
Jad Zughbi**

As He Pointed His Gun Towards Me

As he pointed his gun towards me,
I didn't see flashy memories that came in white,
Myself as a child on a bicycle,
Freshly baked taboon,
The grandmother I didn't know,
A shame they always said:
"She looked like you,"
My mother's red bright face,
My father's big dark eyes.

I saw blood,
I saw red blood coming from my forehead
I saw my body,
Thrown off to the side,
And I worried.

I didn't think of heaven or hell,
I thought of cold freezing coffins,
Lonely nights with no ideas.
Images wanting to explode inside,
For the option of writing is forever lost.

I thought of my brother,
Reading on-line articles while sipping Nescafe,
Hearing about his baby sister,
DEAD,
Left on the road alone.

I thought of the car driver next to me,
As she shifted her body towards the car's door,
I moved mine closer to hers,
Extended my arms,
Offering affection while needing it the most.

I thought of my mother,
Being angry at my recklessness,
Never knowing that I tried to be safe,
Never going to checkpoints to protest,
Suppressing emotions I'll never confess,
I thought of her going to her room, quietly,
Wiping away tears quietly,
Coming out strong quietly.

As he pointed his gun towards me,
I thought of you,
Never allowing your eyes to fill up,
Hiding your sorrow by helping my best friends to cope,
My mother to start cooking again,
My father to stop working night and day,
Visiting places we've never been to,
Just so you won't close your eyes and see me around you.

I thought of my unborn children,
Never knowing how much I'll love them,
Never understanding that each time in life I stumble,
They, their possibility, bring me back to life.

As he pointed his gun towards me,
I never thought of myself,
I thought of them,
My family, Baba and Mama,
Muna and Ibrahim,
I thought of my friends,
The close and the related.

And as he lowered his gun
I exhaled,
I thought of me,
My unwritten words,
My life not lived,
And my undecided future.

Laila Shikaki

Is it a Sin to be Palestinian?

Who is Chris Bandak?

Chris Bandak is a name of a young Palestinian Christian who was born in Bethlehem—Palestine—on Jan. 13, 1979. His first name comes from the holy word, "Christ," and his family name is a well known one among the locals in Bethlehem area. Chris's house is located 2 minutes away from the Nativity Church (the birth place of Jesus Christ) in Bethlehem which was damaged by Israeli soldiers in 2002 during the siege.

Chris Bandak has been in prison in Israel since Feb. 06, 2003 as a result of his patriotism and loyalty to his country—"Palestine"—and friends. Unfortunately, he was charged with 4 life sentences and now praying for his peace and freedom.

I assume that it is easy to talk about Chris; however it is hard to be in his shoes and to live the daily life of a prisoner.

Chris Family Background:

Chris has an older brother called Khader; he is now 31 years old married with 2 children. Chris's mother left her children when they were less than one year old! So at that time the family fell apart and were no living together as family anymore. His father passed away in 2003. Khader and Chris were alone; as a result, they were raised by an angel. Her name is Victoria; she is a relative from their father's side and stayed single all her life looking after the two children. She provided all the basic needs required to have a decent life and saw to it that the boys were educated in excellent schools. She passed away at the age of 90 years old on Mar. 23,2009 and Chris was unable either to see her or say goodbye which left him in deep sorrow and heartbroken inside while in prison.

Chris' life in prison:

Chris is now a second year student majoring in "Political Science and International Relations." Some prisoners are allowed to do that through a joint agreement between the prison management and Hebrew University. He is struggling in prison on his own; only his friends in prison support him. Khader can only visit him once a year ... Imagine!!

Chris is prevented from seeing his nephew and niece. He only sees them through pictures sent by the post office after several procedures of inspection.

In addition to what is said above, I would like to have a further talk about the Israeli Occupation and how it is affecting our daily lives living inside a national prison called PALESTNE.

The Israeli Occupation: No Comments

The Israeli occupation has always been an obstacle for the youth and their future in Palestine for many reasons. First of all, the Segregation Wall is a fine example of the difficulties that we, as Palestinians, face on daily basis. Apart from the checkpoints that are set up between Palestinian cities, there is the intended humiliation and personal insinuation that take place. Second, another obstacle is the settlements and lands. Day by day we are losing the land of Palestine ... it is fading away and the outside world is just watching silently. All this must stop! Till when ... when?!

Moreover, it is important to mention that we as Bethlehemites living in Bethlehem are not allowed to go to Jerusalem unless we apply for a formal permit given by the Israelis. Why? because we are Palestinians? Oh! We are the terrorists, that's right! For God's sake, Jerusalem is 10km away from Bethlehem.

The Israeli repressive measures must cease immediately and Israel must be held accountable for its record in all regards. The measures of colonization must also be stopped and reversed with all the correlating practical and legal ramifications. This occupation must end and the Palestinian people must be allowed to realize their inalienable rights, including the right to establish their own state, so that peace can be achieved on the basis of co-existence and international legalities.

Conclusion

Last but not least, I'm sure now that you have a very good idea about our miserable lives and feelings. I have no doubt that this piece will ring a bell in your minds. But back to our dear brother Chris, at the end of our friendly talk. What Chris truly prays for after spending more than seven years in the Israeli prisons is to meet his only brother, Khader, once again and to live a peaceful life with him and his family . . .

Khader Bandak

Our Beloved Palestine!

With calloused hands and trembling feet,
I looked through the wall cracks
to the other side of the lands.
I saw a shepherd humming
among the olive trees
to entertain his sheep.
There were women and children
chanting in elation:
"Our beloved PALESTINE!
Our land, our hearts and souls."
I tried to chant with them,
but my voice was hoarse
and my soul was dim.
I tried to laugh with them,
but my solitude was grim.
So I stood in reticence
waiting for redemption
from my bleak bitterness.
Palestine is my ultimate relief,
my refuge and my fulfillment.
I will never wave goodbye
to my land again!

Suha Yusef Ilkahil

God Created Life

God created life, planets, universe and Earth with its people. When He created Adam and Eve He made sure to create human beings who would take care of each others, who would live in peace, love each others and protect each other. That's the way God wanted it and still wants the people in the whole world to live.

Being Palestinian is something not easy and that is what I'm so proud about. It's not a coincidence that we (the Palestinian people) live in the middle of the fire's circle. I was born, raised up, and grown mature among the conflict between Israel and Palestine. At the beginning it was scary, shocking and weird. It didn't stop being like that but we got used to it until it became a no other choice issue.

The siege of the Nativity Church was the worst I saw in my life, so far. Seeing people killed, injured, and taken to prison is never easy. Seeing children who were separated from their mothers, hit fiercely, and smashed is never easy either. No food, no school, no way to go out of home, but staying at home in front of the television (If there was electricity) waiting to hear any good news. We had enough time listening to the Israeli soldiers with their weapons and all their war equipment saying "Mamnou' al—tajawool" which means moving or going out of home to any place—even your neighbors—is forbidden and banned.

I remember clearly the image of my aunt cooking in the kitchen when the soldiers saw her through the window and started shooting toward her, on the walls, on the window and on the roof of the house. We were eleven people staying in the same house trying to survive, with less than what should be the minimum life requirements, but the hardest thing was that my dad was not there with us; he was in Italy and couldn't manage to come back as he wasn't allowed, because that time the Israeli army prevented us from traveling around the city. We were not allowed to get out of the country nor come in to it. So we spent our days with my sick old grandmother who needed medicines, my cousins, my uncle and my aunt. These days will never be erased from my memory, but we didn't give up and we will never.

I am a swimmer and I swim; I used to be a champion, during the sieges I always used to go sneaking to the swimming popl as it's located close to our house. I spent really a long time everyday hiding beside the garbage in front of our house whenever I heard the sound of the Jeeps, trucks or the voices of the soldiers, as if I'm doing something wrong and my fault was that I wanted to live my dream of being a talented champion, but I didn't give up as well. Many people I knew, like friends and family members were killed, even the people whom I don't know took a piece of me when they were killed.

I am writing this essay while I'm on my way to Jordan, in order to attend my summer course. I study political science and trying to understand the world's problems and the hidden truth. All I'm seeing on my way to Jordan now is the Israeli checkpoints, which you can find them every 15 minutes, and not forgetting at all the thorough checking of the cars, IDs, the drivers, and the people—especially if they are men. Further more it is tiring to cross the Israeli side on the Allenby Bridge; I guess that it is much easier to reach Europe or USA than to go to Jordan.

Seeing your leader and guide stuck in a room full of sand with no electricity just trying to survive is something sad and downy. President of PLO, Mr. Yasser Arafat, went through all this and never gave up because he believed in our legal case, our freedom and our message. He had no food, no water, no sunlight, nothing. I guess none of the presidents across the whole world will ever accept to be stuck in such situation, not even for few hours, so what if it is few months?! I went to visit Abu Ammar(Yasser Arafat)after they allowed people to go inside the Mokata' after terrible suffering. According to what I saw (the tiny room he was in) not even a homeless person with no house would accept living in it. That's just proves on clear thing: he believed in us, he believed in our case, he believed in his Palestinian people, he believed in us more than we believe in ourselves. No one will handle what he had handled, and that's why he's my model for us to survive our lives.

We have the power to make, choose or create the world we are seeking, but only if we have the courage to make a new beginning, keeping in mind what has been written in:

The Talmud says: "The whole of the Torah is for the purpose of promoting peace."

The Holy Bible tells us: "Blessed are the peacemakers, for they shall be called sons of God."

The Quran says: "We have created you male and female. And we have made you into nations and tribes so that you may know one another."

The people of the world can live together in peace; we know that this is God's vision so now that must be our work here on Earth, to spread love, peace and humanity around the globe.

Maria Asfoura

A Leader is a Dealer in Hope

Did I lose my childhood and my adolescence too? Or I am I losing my youth? These periods in my life ought to have been the most beautiful and precious days, which I should be enjoying. Unfortunately, nothing of this happened. There were no satisfactions during these stages.

I was born on 25th of April 1987. As a child, I gained all the love and kindness from my family. But I did not enjoy it as any child in the world, because after few months from my birth, the First Intifada took place. Days go by and times go fast; minute after minute, hour after hour. And my teenage years have started. Unfortunately, I passed this stage through many challenges.

Since September 2000, the beginnings of the second Intifada, over 3000 people have been killed in the West bank and Gaza Strip; many more were injured or handicapped, and thousands of houses were damaged or destroyed. Daily life has been harshly disrupted by shooting, shelling, curfews, incursions, and by the near impossibility of traveling and transportation, due to the Separation Wall. The closure of the Occupied Palestinian Territories has set off a process of economic decline that touches almost all the Palestinian families. That is a short summary of my teenage years.

At that time, Life was precious for me, and for every person who is suffering. Carrying on with your life wasn't easy, and life became a difficult dilemma that no one can understand. Although, trying to be optimistic and continue living our life was a daily struggle for us, we were obliged to do that because life goes on with or without. The occupation did not break my own dream; because I believe that future belongs to those who believe in the beauty of their dreams.

Everyone has a vision, a message, and responsibilities in his life. Even a minor player can change a whole society. Through facing these challenges, I did not give up. I can see the future in everything I do. I can see it in my studying, in my tolerance to live, to express myself, and by being proud of my identity.

I finished studying at school in 2005, after that I attend Bethlehem University. It was a new beginning in my life. I was an activist and a member in the student senate. I believe that youth are the influential part in their communities. In various social, political, cultural, and legal contexts, the word "youth" refers to a predetermined set of experiences, ideas, and perspective. Youth is the most worthy treasure in every community which the community has to think about and maintain. If the community loses it's youth power, it will go down. Therefore, for me, to be a young leader and an influential person is a great step. This means that I can be responsible and an independent person. The principal goal of attending these activities is to create leaders who are capable of doing new things, not simply of repeating what other generations have done.

Today, I'm one of the Young Political Leaders who believe in the necessity of the change. To live in peace is the main purpose, which must be achieved. The new generation is looking for a new method of living. They want to find peace and security. They still have hope that Peace will exist one day in the Middle East. The struggle between the Palestinians and the Israelis must be ended. Our future must differ from our childhood, teenage, and even our present. The next generations must live in peace. And it's our responsibility toward our country to find a solution.

Palestinians and Israelis are different communities and have dissimilar cultures and thoughts. They have been fighting for many years to have control over the Holy Lands. The principal goal for each side is to kick out the other side. The absence of communicating and understanding each others for a long time empowers discrimination between both communities. So, it's time to begin and create a new relation. Youth must not wait for leaders to begin; they must do it alone, person to person. To become a member of change, it's the only thing that will remain constant. Youth's duties may be finished some day, thought its results will never. As a result, having exchange programs and joint conferences have become necessary in our current living, in order to cease the misunderstanding and to be unbiased among others. Discussing the rising issues on the political stage, making efforts to find solutions for these conflicts, and passing it through the new generation are a part of young leaders' responsibilities toward their countries to help spread awareness and knowledge among their people.

To sum up, our visions begin with our desires; step by step young leaders can create a world full of peace, sympathy and acceptance toward the others. Rights can never be lost, stolen, measured, bought or sold; they must be given freely. We have to be optimists and find opportunities in everything we do.

Rawan Hayek Jadallah

I am not an I.D

In Jerusalem, I am identified with my blue I.D.
As if the color defines me
What they don't know is that I am more than what they call me
I am Palestinian and more than an I.D.

The tax in Jerusalem is very costly
Checkpoints, humiliation and repression are what I go through
daily
Please don't envy the outward of me
Because in Jerusalem, they don't even admit my nationality

To end my story briefly
I need to remind you of the true me
I am human, I am a Jerusalemite, and I am not an I.D.
I am Palestine and Palestine lives within me.

Aya Khashan

I dream 24h/day!

About 8,000 prisoners in the Israeli jails . . . if not more . . . and you are one of them. They arrested you two years ago. But until today they did not judge you. They keep on postponing the court. Are they going to imprison you for a decade and then they might think about judging you?

It is hard to recount all the things that are absent since your departure; that makes you more present than ever. The walls of our house are not white any more but gray. The windows do not open anymore. Our door bell rarely rings. And I dream 24 hours a day about you being here. I smile for anything and anything makes me cry.

You look fifty rather that twenty eight. Makeup makes me look my age; twenty four, it hides my fifties too.

I have been trying to contact this radio program for prisoners—the only means of communication with you, when it is not being behind a protected glass—but, lots of pressure. I am not the only one who wants to say take care! And I hope you & all the prisoners will get out soon!

Dina Al-Halayka

Living Under Occupation

Life under occupation—Where do I begin! It feels like Dr. Hannah Musleh described it in one of his documentaries, as falling into the Spider's Web.

I am a 23 year old woman, from Beit Jala. I studied Business Administration at Bethlehem University, and I currently work as a Public Relations officer at the Arab Educational Institute in Bethlehem. As my age indicates, I was born in the first Intifada in 1987.

Born in the first intifada, was raised in the period of all the peace agreements, and found my adult years to begin with the second intifada. So I guess we can omit the word *normal* childhood out of my life, as my first word when I was 9 months came out at a checkpoint, where I proudly shouted PLO!

There are so many stories about living under occupation which is why it is so difficult to actually choose one. I have so many memories of many incidents, but I thought I will focus on the most recent, with the hope that spreading the word about it might make a change.

I live in Beit Jala, on top of the mountain where my parents started building our home in 1978, and where we are blessed with a beautiful view of the mountains, perfect breeze, and a gorgeous environment where you can relax, meditate and enjoy the countryside away from the noises. That is why it has been under the eye of the Israeli occupation for so long—their tactics having started 1967. By placing both settlements of Gilo and Har Gilo on top of the mountains surrounding Beit Jala—these actions continued throughout the years—that whenever anything happened around

Palestine and Israel, the road where we live was blocked from all sides, creating checkpoints at every entrance to town.

Years passed, and in 1994 we received the first confiscation orders for the family lands. It said that a bypass road would be opened and that it would pass through our lands. Of course we rejected the order, and we tried to stop it. But there was nothing we could do about it. The Israeli bulldozers came and started digging and working, and since it is a mountain with many heavy rocks, they had to use dynamite to open the road! And with every explosion, our home shook from every corner, rocks flew and broke the windows and doors, and our floors, are, until this day, not flat! We were never compensated for the damages nor the land, and in return we are not even to come close or pass through the road, which is now called the Tunnel Road—Road 60 that leads to Jerusalem.

Then, the calmness that outran the storm came to an end—The Second Intifada irrupted! Fighting quickly shifted from Jerusalem, to Beit Jala and the once tranquil town was interrupted by the bombs and missiles that fell into the homes of the people. With the excuse that the settlements were shot at by Palestinians, the heavy raid and invasions around Beit Jala and Bethlehem area in general were getting worse by the day. The collective punishment which Israel is well known for left people in a state of disbelief, shattered, and afraid for their lives. Many people left their homes and immigrated, others lost their homes in the shootings (in fact 1100 homes were destroyed), some lost loved ones (*Beit Jala lost 5 martyrs, who were killed in their homes and none of them were part of the fighting*) and others had to deal with and still dealing with traumatic effects on their children.

From 2000 till 2004, the road that I live in was blocked by dirt checkpoints and we were not allowed to pass with a car. We had to park somewhere outside the road, and walk to our homes, and every dirt checkpoint had a tower filled with Israeli soldiers that stopped us on the way. No one could reach us, for four years; if you had an emergency the ambulance couldn't reach you; if anything needed to be fixed—telephone, electricity or water pipes—the companies had to make an arrangement and get a permit to reach you. Things were getting more horrible as the days passed so bad, that one of our neighbors, Jacob Sansour had a heart attack one night, and not only didn't the Israeli soldiers let the ambulance pass but they ordered him to walk to another checkpoint. Jacob passed away that day, before he even reached the hospital.

We clearly have had enough. My family hired a lawyer and we went to court after signing a petition from all 94 neighbors living on that road, and We won! The checkpoint was supposed to be open all the time, but just to harass us more they opened it from 7 A.M to 7 P.M., stopping people for long hours before letting them pass, and telling us if we didn't like the treatment, we should find another place to live! But we were determined to open the road, and we did. The road was later opened for 24 hours, but with the presence of the Israeli soldiers around.

In 2005, the future turned black again. We received a confiscation order of the lands surrounding our home—oh yes, we are now a threat to the security of road 60; the same road which they opened from our land! And the Apartheid Wall must pass from in front of our home and block the air from all three sides, forcing us to live in a box! We were outraged. Every now and then they used the security excuse, but it was clear that they just wanted the land. So we were determined to take action, and we hired another lawyer, and he managed to shift the wall so that instead of coming 5 meters away from our home, it was arranged to be 20 meters below. However, we are still unsure of the future of the place, as Israel keeps on changing the maps and the routes as it wants. Recently, we received a new confiscation order, saying it's for the route of the wall, but it is not clear where the wall will pass; that's why we are currently in a state of panic! We are worried, as rumor has it, that they will apply the old plan again.

I am terribly worried that I will be a prisoner for the rest of my life, living in a tomb. Not only, will the Wall confiscate all the lands, but every concrete wall, has a tower with soldiers, barbed wires, and cameras. Moreover, it will mean that we cannot be on top of the roof of the house; we cannot build and cannot expand. And as the Israeli lexicon has translated the non violent resistance into "terror," lands confiscating will be translated into "security reasons", and the soldiers' harassments into "they had to." I cannot help but be frustrated.

The Apartheid Wall has zigzagged its way into people's lives deep into the West Bank and not even close to the green line.

It has affected and is still affecting every aspect of our lives. People who depend on agriculture for a living cannot reach their lands, they can no longer farm nor harvest their crops, and their former source of income is now no longer accessible. Beit Jala alone had lost 72% of its lands because of the Apartheid Wall, settlements, and bypass roads for the settlers. From 14680 acres, what is left now is 4190 acres. The transformation of Beit Jala into a Ghetto, has increased the numbers of immigrants, in fact 125,000 people have left Beit Jala since Al Nakba (the Palestinian catastrophe) in 1948. And unfortunately the number is still increasing, as more people, especially the young, are leaving the area.

That is why I am sharing my story with you, with the hope that we can make a change. From one human being to the other, I encourage you to learn the story of the other side, the side that Israel always tries to cover.

We are not terrorists with a death wish; we are human beings who want to live. And as a person, who believes in the power of the people I leave my story with you, hoping that you will keep in mind that: *"Injustice anywhere, is a threat to justice everywhere."* Dr. Martin Luther King Jr.

Raneen Al-Arja

In Palestine

In Palestine
Life tastes different
I don't expect you to understand
Because you can't see the magic
my eyes were born to see

In every inch of the land
A story lies behind
A drop of blood and a bullet
Sun only rises to bring another hope
And with a kiss . . .
We leave our beloved
For it might be the last goodbye

In Palestine
Air is measured
And sun is covered . . . by a wall
A wall that isn't built to shelter
But to create suffering

As humans
We choose freedom
In this holy land
We seek strength from the greatest mountains

And wisdom form the deepest seas
I place Palestine next to my heart

For our pulses
And the blood running in our veins is one
A land that gives birth to martyrs
Will not be stained with shame
A land touched by God's hand
will be free one day

In Palestine
Death is a tradition
a celebration of a promised gift
Freedom stolen by an evil hand
and will be restored by God's will

In Palestine
We cry the Olive
Fight with a stone
To break the chains of injustice
Right of existence is a liberty
Killing children is legal
A potential terrorist needs to be destroyed

In Palestine
Resistance is a crime

And a demolished house is the price
Water is a luxury we need to beg for
All weapons are legal
Targets we are considered
And behind bars
We are forced to stand

In Palestine
Values are deformed with a gun
Pride is a product
We aren't allowed to consume
And human rights
is a red line we should not cross.

In Palestine
Time is not on our side
It was taken decades ago
And there it is . . . lying behind a green line
A line that forces us all into one raped future

Here in Palestine
Red is the blood
Green is the land
Black is the rage
And white . . .
White is the peace we once dreamed of
And now stands an illusion.

Raneen Al-Arja

If Only Walls Could Talk

Walking through the old city of Jerusalem, the evening prayers of the mosque, the bells of the church ringing loud and clear! People rushing around for their daily chores!

You can see the amazing diversity of religion and race, and just think of what a special place it is to be in that particular exact moment!

The deeper the walk gets into the heart of Jerusalem the closer it gets to feel the heartbeat of the walls pounding with history and eager to tell stories . . . If only walls can talk . . .

The smells of fresh ka`ek, falafel, Arabic coffee, and the taste of hummus through both Christian and Islamic quarters. The freshly baked lahmajun (Armenian pizza) spreading through the Armenian quarter, and the melody of Pizmonim (traditional Hebrew songs) around the Jewish quarter!

Each stone has its own story to state, from the beginning of time starting with the Canaanite period to the Roman empire all the way to the Umayyad Caliphate and throughout the crusaders, Ottoman empire till the present that is called Palestine/Israel.

They are looking forward to meet the other newcomers that are yet to come in order to pass it on to the next generation—for someday our present shall become the history in our future. It is believed that every nation and power rise and fall which was witnessed by these walls and narrow stretching roads of the old city in Jerusalem during different kinds of eras that came across this city in days gone by.

It is known that different people from diverse backgrounds and religions have bases in Jerusalem, with every authority or ruler, new people came, hence adding some culture of their own bonding with the existing one already; some of them stayed, some of them left. However it is noticed that there is a glance of hope of peaceful coexistence! When a journey is taken around the seven gates of Jerusalem, the footprints of every community have left behind are visible, still walking side by side peacefully amongst each other: Palestinians, Assyrians, Greeks, Turks, Jews, Armenians, and Jordanians .... Although they have different backgrounds, religions, and (some of them) languages, they have a way of living together in harmonious peace even if the political rulers keep changing that harmony. For instance, the current political ruler, trying to separate each community from the other, puts up stream barriers every once in a while through the old city, enact new sets of laws that are applied on minority communities or the Arab society and not on others, yet that doesn't stop the strong connections that the streets of Jerusalem have, for at each crossroad, societies collide with a greeting to one another, there is interaction and communications between one another no matter what background or religion the other person might hold, friendships throughout the years have been formed with one another, from one generation to the next whether it began through businesses or simply for the sake of knowing the other, far away from any political rule and most of them don't want to change this bond. Moreover, no law can separate this kind of interaction since people would like to live in tranquility and hope that someday they will walk side by side all the way through the old roads of Jerusalem with no restrictions whatsoever.

Nanor Arakelian

The Only Memories Left About My Hometown, Jaffa

It's been 62 years and yet she still remembers it with every minor detail. Maybe because that day marks their loss of land, home and sense of belonging. "Al—Nakba (the Catastrophe) is the harshest experience that I have ever been through," my grandmother said. "It is too hard to lose everything in one single day, when the very day before you think you have a perfect life."

Al—Nakba marks the evacuation of people from their own houses and homeland. It marks people's suffering and misery. It marks the day when families went homeless and lost everything. Many villages were totally destroyed along with the death of their inhabitants. My grandmother said, "It makes me feel very sad when I remember all these villages that no longer exist; their inhabitants were slaughtered like animals." "It makes me even more miserable when I see that these villages are lost from our memories. "Forgive me for I keep telling you about this horrible incident, but these are the only memories which are left to remind me of my home town and beloved Jaffa".

Julia Marianne, the daughter of Jubran and Zahieh Marianne, was born in Jaffa in1930. She lived there among her three sisters and two brothers; she told me that she had a nearly perfect life. She still remembers Al—Ajami Street quite well even though it's been decades since the last time she has been there. She still remembers her friends, relatives and school. However, these blissful moments were very short. It all started in 1948; rumors spread among the people that Israel was going to take over the city. It was not so long ago when the Israeli Army began its maneuvers in the city. "It was very brutal," she said. "We used to hide in underground shelters and in lanes in order to survive." Every time they heard the bombardment they used to leave their houses under the bombs to flee to shelters. It was hard circumstances in shelters with the sounds of bombardment mixed with the sound of the juveniles weeping. "I used to feel very insecure when I saw the looks of fear in the parent's eyes. Their looks of fear made me feel that we were in great danger. It was even harder when we got out of shelters to see whose houses were demolished. It was moments of great melancholy when I saw men and women crying over their destroyed houses. Women used to pass out, children used to search for their remaining toys." Days passed; the shelters seemed insufficient for them to survive. Once, during a maneuver, down in the shelter, everybody was very frustrated as if they knew that something dreadful was going to happen. My grandmother saw the feelings of fear and despair in the eyes of the those hiding in the shelter; it was not so long afterward when she could no longer see these people. She heard a great crash; she closed her eyes because she was in a great fear. The sounds of bombardment and destruction sounded very close; still she did not open her eyes. Then when she opened them to make sure that her family was alive, she beheld the great destruction in front of her. The Israelis had bombarded the shelter. My grandmother, along her family, managed to get out alive, unlike a lot who were stuck during the attack. It was a near death experience; young children were crying because they lost their parents; mothers were wandering around searching for their children. It was disastrous.

People were overcome from the war. Some lost their houses, others their lives. It was a tragedy, literally. Fleeing to secure their lives and their children's lives was not a bad idea at the time, especially when Israel started to attack houses, forcing people to leave. People were in great fear, particularly when they heard the massacres in the nearby villages. "We kept wondering when it will be our turn to be killed," my grandmother uttered. Israel convinced the people in Jaffa to surrender their keys and flee for two weeks only in order to secure their lives. However, they assured them that after two weeks they could come back to have their keys and live a peaceful life. People took whatever furniture they were able to carry and left. "As for us, we took my sister's sewing machine and left to a nearby village," my grandmother said. After two weeks people started to return to their houses. My grandmother was extremely happy to return to live a peaceful life again. "We were more than thrilled to return; unfortunately it was not as we anticipated at all. We were astonished to see that there were Israeli families settling in our houses. This was the greatest anguish of all; they were our homes with our heritage, pictures, clothes, furniture. How could they rip off our lives from us?" my grandmother asked. People were hysterical; It was clear that they had lost everything. Everybody started leaving. My grandmother's family chose to flee to Jordan. They left in trucks, crowded with many people, among what they could save from their furniture. Everyone was silent in the trucks; there was nothing to say. Some cried secretly. They could not look at each other in the eye. Leaving in the truck their silence was disturbed by great screams from the sea side; they all looked there and saw a man pushing his three young daughters in the sea and stood there until he was sure they were dead. He was screaming that they were better off dead. This man could not leave Jaffa and wanted to be sure that his daughters died with honor; he was afraid that the Israeli soldiers would rape them. They raped a whole country; they could do anything.

The path to Jordan was very painful. There were so many thoughts crossing my grandmother's head. She kept asking herself, "would she be able to enter her home again? To see her old clothes, books . . ." The concerns and apprehensions were amplified when they left the trucks at night to find somewhere to sleep. They slept that night in an animal inn. It was ironic' it had been just a few days since they had slept in their big houses and fancy beds, and here they were sleeping on the floor in an inn where animals might have thought it was no longer suitable for them.

However, they had to move on. It was very hard in Jordan because they had nothing. But her sister's sewing machine had a great effect on their lives. Her sister started working and was the only provider for the family at first. "The harsh conditions in Jordan took over our thoughts," my grandmother said, "but we never forgot about our homeland". Months passed, my grandmother got married, and moved with her husband to Bethlehem—Palestine.

It was many years later when my grandmother returned to visit Jaffa. She went directly to her house; it was still there as she left it.

With her sister she approached their house and saw the Israelis who had settled in it. They pleaded with them to enter but their endeavors were rejected. They got depressed, but she told me that at least they got the chance to see her old home again. My grandmother told me that she had mixed feelings; she felt that she had gained and lost a part of herself at the same time. She felt that she was restored by seeing a house she has craved many years to see, and lost because she knew that her house was no longer hers.

Many years later, my grandmother got the chance to go, once more, to Jaffa, but this visit was totally unpleasant. She went to Al—Ajami Street but many changes had taken place in the city. She went to see her house-just from the outside; it would give her momentary relief, as she told me. However, she was extremely shocked when she saw that her house was demolished; she could not see anything but destruction. The only remaining thing was a piece of wood that was left from the water mill. It brought a lot of unpleasant memories. She looked at it and cried. She was extremely sad thinking that if they were planning to demolish it why would they take it over and settle in it. "This moment kills every hope that we will return one day to Jaffa," my grandmother said.

Years passed. My grandmother lived her life with her husband and kids. The burdens of life took over her thoughts. Now she keeps thinking about the place she wants to be buried in. Should it be Jordan among her parents, or should it be Jaffa? She keeps asking herself if it was the right decision to leave 62 years ago in order to survive, or should they have stayed there and died as martyrs? "It is really hard to tell if I deserve to be buried in Jaffa, the city that we abandoned."

By Raghda Da'boub

My New Birthday

I am considered to be one of the third generation of the Palestinian Nakba (catastrophe). It's a constant memory and an occasion we commemorate on May 14, the same day which Israel celebrates its state establishment. Before 1948, there was no state of Israel, but history is unpredictable; it added to its decomposed documents the flourishing state of Israel. In one decision in the Untied Nation, the history stated the establishment of a new country on the land of another's people country.

On that day, May 14th, 1948, the Zionist dream became true with the support of more than 50 countries around the world. They all agreed on the partition resolution of 1947 and with this process these countries ignored the real inhabitants of the land and ignored their right to decide their own destinies. The partition was created to protect the Jews who were the new immigrants to the land after the racism they faced in Europe, especially after the Holocaust which the native Palestinian farmers had no relationship with in any way, shape or form. But they were honored for their peaceful ways of living by being ethnically cleansed, uprooted from their lands, and having a new history written for them by the Israelis.

Today, the ignored population is over ten million individuals. Less than four million of them live inside Palestine and most of them are refugees from destroyed villages in 1948 and 1967. The rest of the population is dispersed in uncertain host countries like Lebanon which is not willing to give a residency certificate to the Palestinian refugees. So, who are they? What is their identity? Why do they have to live in this long and never-ending temporary status? This temporary status will always be a reminder of the need to live in permanence, to return to their roots, to where they are originally from.

Now I feel that I am a very lucky person. I never felt that lucky before the day of my new birthday, the day I visited my original destroyed village of "Deir Rafat," ("Regina Palestina" which means "Queen of Palestine") where my grandfather and his family lived before they were kicked out and forced to leave.

From that day I started my history and my new life. I was very scared at the beginning as I approached the Israeli soldiers at the checkpoints even though that I had a permit to enter Jerusalem. These feelings of fear vanished the moment I reached some of the destroyed villages of my friend's families and neighbors. Driving from Dheisheh refugee camp, crossing the checkpoint and entering the land of 1948 make me feel as if I am in a different country: the green trees, fresh air, no houses, and beautiful landscapes that I have not seen in many countries that I have visited around the world.

Things changed dramatically inside me when I saw the "Deir Rafat" sign on the left side of the road. I could feel my heart beat within each part of my body. I could not wait anymore, I wanted to jump from the car and stand on the land. I wanted to scream loudly "This is my village ... I am from here," so that everyone on this earth could hear me.

Now, I see everything like a movie playing repeatedly in my head over and over again. It is like a painted mural in front of me. I could not believe that this was my village. The pictures that I have drawn in my mind from the stories my grandfather have told me, are nothing compared to the beautiful scenes my eyes were observing.

When I left the car and walked in the monastery, I got a feeling I had never had before, a feeling when your heart is empty and something is filling it. I did not know exactly what this feeling was until now! I was discussing within myself that two eyes were not enough for me at that moment. I needed and wanted more eyes so that I could see the whole village all the time. We went down the valley behind the monastery. We saw a destroyed well; the village had nine wells as my grandfather told me. It was heartbreaking when I saw that the well is dumped with garbage; it should be beautiful and clean with drinking water.

We continued by the car to see olive and cactus gardens, on both sides of the small roads. Cactus and olives trees are signs of life and inhabitants in that area. We proceeded a bit farther, walking and we saw some Bedouins tents and their livestock. We climbed a little bit of the hill and some ruins of the village emerged. We saw a very nice arc on the hill; I think this arc is part of a destroyed house Inside me my heart was filled with strange feelings and my mind was going back and forth between Deir Rafat and Dheisheh. Why can't my family and I live here in Deir Rafat peacefully? Why can't my grandfather come back to his land to planet his olive trees as he used to do with his father before July 18, 1948?

I lay down on one of the ruined walls of a house and kept watching the blue clear sky; at that moment I felt that the sky is very close. I wanted to hide in it, to stay in Deir Rafat. I was breathing the air again and again as if I could not have enough of it.

I collected some flowers and Za'atar baladi. We took the car again, drove back towards the well, continued to the other side where there were more of the olive trees on both sides, and we saw a tent with Bedouins in it. We headed there; the woman invited us to enter, she knew some of my family relatives, and she also told us that they pay NIS 2000 every 20 days to Biet Sham'sh Municipality for the tent they live in. I will pay everything and anything to live there, while I should be living there since forever. Instead am living in a zoo and struggling for my basic rights.

At the end, I got the flowers I brought with me from Bethlehem; I planted three near the well. One for my grandfather's father. Another for my grandfather and one for my family. My village is already gorgeous and my flowers will not add any beauty to it. I don't put them there because I will return after 20 years to claim an ownership for the land, where I planted three flowers. I own the land now and I owned it then, I do not need any evidence. I planted them as a gift to the land I loved even before we met and as my guide to the light at the end of the tunnel. I hope my land liked the gift.

It's time to wake up from the real dream, time to go back to Dheisheh Refugee Camp, which I like, but do not belong to. Its time to face my family; they were all anxious to know how home looked like, where exactly did I go. I couldn't reply more than that it's the most beautiful place I have ever seen in my life.

I got frustrated after all that joy; my mother wanted so much to come and visit, to see the village. Till this moment I cannot meet my grandfather, who has a lot of memories in Deir Rafat, childhood memories, his house, his mother's grave, his youthful times and yet, he cannot go there to visit and I went, it is just an unfair world.

Areej Jafari

Dreaming of a House

The lack of freedom and justice is the reason behind writing my words today. I could be, someday, just a reader for someone who could be in my place. When I was born I was breathing air like all human beings did, I drank water from the sources of this earth, but today I do not need more than human rights for others and for myself. We all share the land; the earth is our small home in this large universe. I spend so much time thinking how much life would be better if we lived all together, though we are many, but we could be one body. These are not fancy ideas; they are inside each one of us. I do not know why there are a lot of children suffering and dying from food and water shortages, but I still see hope in their eyes because they know that they are not alone, they know that we are humans and we help each other.

I never thought my family and I would be affected directly by the occupation; I never thought this will be a reason for me today to write these words. I still remember all those years with my family while we were moving from one place to another. Those years when we did not own a house. I even still remember my family dreams about building a house until our dreams became true. We built our first house finally without knowing that it would be a beginning to our dreams again. We lived in that house, on our piece of land only for three years until the Israeli court started sending papers asking us to have permission for our house. It seems logical and legal to get a permit to keep our sweet home home. Our house's area is under the Palestinian Authority; we take all our services from the Palestinian authority. We cannot reach Jerusalem even if we want to apply for entry permission. When they took my father to the Israeli court the judge said I cannot judge you upon Israeli laws as you do not have an Israeli ID because you do not live under our authority, but after struggling for three years they charged us twenty-five thousand US $, which is a huge amount of many for my family to afford and we would not like to pay even if we had this amount. The last decision was demolishing our house. We lived in a tent for three months in winter. My brother and I were going to our schools. Life became more and more difficult. People finally decided to rebuild our home again at the same place and having the same size. They collected money and started working, Palestinians and Israelis together, hand by hand. They were against the unfairness of the Israeli government regulations. We thought that we got our house back again without knowing that we just went back to the zero point. Just after fifteen days the same people returned but this time they brought new reason for us—that the wall would be built where our home is built. We went back to the same frustrating situation. We even thought that the business of the first home was finished with its demolition but even after the first month of living in the second house they sent us the first fine for the first house plus the demolishing cost. We went back to the court which means we just returned to the unfairness again. We are not against laws and I am not asking only to look at this case with a human viewpoint only. They want the land with no people. We are living in the Palestinian part as I said and the Israelis deal with us as if we are living under their control when they are talking about the land but they deal with us as people who are living under the Palestinian Authority when talking about rights and services.

After eight months in the second house, that morning they woke us with another demolishing again. They asked us to go out; they threw everything outside the house and demolished our beloved home and shelter again. I know many people who think that the Israeli government does not make these things or even they think my family and I are bad people so they demolished our home as if we deserve that. I still remember each moment my parents spent to develop our minds and planting the seeds of peace in our heart. As we believe in peace and as we never lose hope we found many people around us—not only Palestinian and Israeli—but also from many countries who traveled from their counties to rebuild our house again for the third time. I think they not only built Palestinian houses demolished by the Israeli government but also they chose peace, justice and they believe in helping humans—not hurting others as the Israeli government did with my family. My family and I remember how people rebuilt our house and we forgot that our house were demolished.

I do not know why the Israeli government is above the laws always. I do not need more than applying laws and human rights. I was happy when I heard that the International Court of Justice issued a decision to stop building the wall but when I became older I understood that the Israeli government will stop building the wall after they finish the last part of it, after they take all these lands and demolish all the houses built on it. They separated people; they surrounded the place where our Lord Jesus Christ was born. I do not know why there is a wall built in the Holy Land—not a bridge between people. The wall prevented people on both sides from getting any chance to talk or meet. I know that they say that the wall is built under security reasons but it's logical to think that people can climb ten meters high or use underground tunnels. I do not know how could a wall protect the Palestinians from the Israeli air strikes or bring peace to both the Israelis and the Palestinians. Anyway the problem with the wall is its location as it's not on the '67 borders but it's built on the Palestinian borders, which means that the wall was built on Palestinian lands. I always hear about the negotiations between the both governments that always suggest a two states solution. I am neither with nor against this solution, but I'm thinking logically with some reality about how they can make a two states solution and in the West Bank there are many settlements surrounding each Palestinian city. Would the Israeli government try stop controlling the Dead Sea area or the cities inside the West Bank like the old city of Hebron for example? I do not know why people believe in lies and close their eyes hiding from bitter realities. I believe that both parts should work for the benefit of their people and the others as well so that we can live in a peaceful Holy Land.

Almuataz Salem

Palestine . . .

Is a boy losing his joy

A girl losing her toy

Is that Palestine?

Fine

Palestine . . .

Is a child

While playing on the sand

Being shot on his own land

Palestine

It's where we are born . . . we live . . . But immediately die

Where our hearts are filled with sorrow and despair

Palestine

Bloodshed . . . and rocks

Children in tombs

Those innocent children whose dreams fade away while their
nightmares come true

Yet

They do not complain

Instead

They are put in chains

You are insane

For making them suffer their pain

Palestine . . .

Is a word that Arabs can't spell

Whether it exists or not . . . they can't tell

In the trap . . . they fell

And it's hard to get them out . . . who will?

Even if we scream . . . they pretend not to hear

Our fear is real

We bear . . . tear after tear

For our freedom to be near

Palestine . . .

Is a smile . . . but a cry

To live ... but to die

Moments to cheer ... years to sigh

This is

Palestine ...

By: Doa Mansour

Freedom of Expression

25 June 2010

The Palestinian territories are characterized by the security control of several parties which leads to a multiplicity of actors that violates media freedoms. There are Israeli occupation authorities and settlers on the one hand and security apparatuses in the West Bank and the Gaza Strip on the other, in addition to the Palestinian groups which led to the continued decline of media freedom and freedom of expression. The excessive practice of self censorship by journalists and media outlets have also led to a decline in the level and professionalism of Palestinian media.

In the first five months of this year, the Palestinian Center for Development and Media Freedoms (MADA) has monitored 80 violations against journalists in occupied Palestinian territories. 67 of them were committed by the Israeli side, and the other were committed by the Palestinian side.

The Israeli occupation forces committed 26 violations against journalists during their coverage of the peaceful marches in the West Bank during the same period. The occupation forces are trying to prevent the journalists from covering the march events by different ways, such as beating, detaining, arresting, and bombing gas grenade on them.

The journalists are paying a high price for their hard insistence on covering the peaceful marches in the West Bank. APA and Wafa Agencies photographer Muammar Jameel Awad (25 years old), was injured by a gas bomb to his head while he was covering a peaceful march in the city of Biet Jala. The photographer's health condition was very precarious, where he was injured with a large wound in his head, and wasn't able to work for more than 2 weeks.

Palestine TV correspondent Haroon Amyreh, who had suffered from several violations by the Israeli occupation forces since the beginning of this year said: "The violations have a positive and negative impact on the Journalist; the positive effect is that it increases the insistence of the Journalist to convey the truth to the whole world, and it gives him a greater motivation to continue covering the events, despite all the risks. The negative effect is the feeling that there is no lasting security, where the beatings and insults by the Israeli occupation forces become as a routine for me."

On 20 June 2010 six journalists were attacked by Israeli forces in Biet Jala. Pal Media cameraman Yousef Shaheen who was one of them said that he was standing with a group of journalists to cover the weekly march events in Biet Jala, and during their coverage, a group of Israeli soldier approached, cursed, and beat them with sticks on their legs, causing him and some of his colleagues bruises in their legs.

"The journalists were directly targeted, where the soldiers left the demonstrators and began to curse and beat us brutally with sticks, causing physical harm to most of the journalists who were in the place," commented another journalist who was also was attacked.

Article 19 of The Universal Declaration of Human Rights that was adopted by the General Assembly of the United Nations in 1984 guarantees the right of freedom of expression: "Everyone has the right to freedom of opinion and expression; this right includes freedom to hold opinions without interference and to seek, receive and impart information and ideas through any media and regardless of frontiers." In spite of that, the Palestinian journalists are being deprived of their right of the freedom of expression, and also have been subjected to much harassment during their work by the Israeli occupation forces. No one succeeds in holding the Israeli government accountable for its continuous violations of freedom of expression, including the human rights organizations and media freedoms defenders

Despite the seriousness of the situation in the Palestinian territories and the magnitude of the repeated attacks on them, the Palestinian journalists continue to do their full duty, risking their lives in many cases. The redeeming feature here, the bright spot, is that many of them have received regional and international awards which indicate their high level of professionalism.

Rihean Abu Aita

Life After the Wall

During the previous years before the Intifada (uprising) began, my family and I used to live in peace and safety, in our own home. Our home is located in one of the most vibrant and active areas in Bethlehem, a neighborhood called Rachel's Tomb. This area is located at the entrance to Bethlehem. Formerly, a peaceful place, it has turned into a dead, war zone.

I. Arlette Anastas, and my husband, George Anastas, are a Palestinian Christian family from Bethlehem. We have four daughters and one son, all together living in building opposite Rachel's Tomb, and surrounded by a nine meter wall on three sides, so that leaves us only one side open and sun, barely, can come through it. As we live nearby Rachel's Tomb our house is subjected to a tough and severe military measures. Although we have some shops located on the first stage which overseeing the street, we can't get good use of them since they are closed, so no business plans could be made in front of our house.

It was well known during the past good years that this main street which is an entrance that leads to Bethlehem city is the richest and liveliest areas in Bethlehem. People used to come from all over the cities to shop at the stores here. But now it is a dead, imprisoned, and scary zone. As my home is left alone with no neighbors surrounding us, the nine meter wall surrounding us makes us feel like we are buried alive in a very dark place.

During the years of the second Intifada we had much pressure and stress and in the year 2002 there was a lot of shooting and clashes. With our house being in a high position we lived in a cross fire field. Our house was occupied by the Israeli soldiers and the shooting toward our house came from different directions. That made my kids paralyzed from the great fear spread among them.

During the shooting there were times bullets entered forcefully into our house, we didn't know whereto hide, what to do, nor where to go. This situation lasted for one terrible year.

It is horrible to live our life with a nine meters wall surrounding us on three sides. My children suffered a lot due to this, they feel like they don't have any future after the erection of this wall in one day.

What mostly bothered me is that I couldn't defend my home nor my family. I couldn't even do anything to help. Later I started to have bad feelings and tightness about almost everything: life, work, and everything regarding how the wall effects our life.

After the construction of the wall which isolated my house from the outer world, my children were shocked; they were even afraid to go outside and look at it. One day I left home for Jerusalem at 6:00am in the morning because of the checkpoints, but when I came back, I was shocked by the view of the new wall horrible and awful. That day I started crying and asked my husband about what was going on around us. He told me that the men building the wall had worked hard to get it done so quickly. I was shocked for two months, but finally managed to get my strength and kept going on for the sake of my children, the eldest of whom, Amanda, remembers how the wall destroyed her life when she was 14 years old. She wanted to do many things but couldn't find an open door to walk though to the outer world, and she still feels sad and depressed due to this giant ugly wall. My younger daughter whose age is 18 years now remembers how we are all psychologically harmed after the building of the segregation wall. She said that she can't feel any joy in us (her parents), not even within herself. She feels that there's no peace and that her house is located in dark, dead area. She worries about her future and what will happen when she finishes school.

We love our home and our city, and no matter how high the wall could be; we will never leave our beloved hometown, because of this wall. It's our place, the place where Jesus was born and we are lucky to live here, because this place should be the place of peace & love instead of building walls.

After all this, I started to think of my children's future. So, I began with an on-line business, which is about making garments for the baptism of the infants and started selling them on-line using the Internet to reach the Christians around the world, since some people do really appreciate these baptism garments as they were made in Holy Bethlehem, where Jesus was born.

So as you see, I didn't give up Hope, and I went from being shocked and stuck in a terrible situation, to being angry, but after a while I started working in a better way to save our future.

Arlette Anastas

Life Under Occupation

Who am I? That's a question that anyone could ask, and it might be easy for you to answer. However, for me it may be different. Should I firstly identify myself by religion? Or should I start by mentioning my nationality? Most of the people from the West think that all Arabs are Muslims, and that's really ironic because the Arab nationality isn't specifically just for Muslims! So, for me, a Palestinian Christian "Arab" living in the city of Bethlehem? Unlike other towns or cities in the West Bank and Gaza strip, currently, Bethlehem isn't undergoing daily invasions or week long curfews imposed by Israel, though the Israeli soldiers come in and out of Bethlehem on a daily basis. But the Israeli occupation is still very visible in many ways. On one hand, The Apartheid Wall (Separation Wall) has a big effect on Bethlehem city because not many pilgrims traveling to Bethlehem are able to reach the city where Jesus was born because of the check points and many other obstacles. Moreover, the local population, who are forbidden to enter Jerusalem without permits, have great difficulties in getting to work, visiting relatives, going to schools or universities, and even getting emergency treatment in hospitals. Moreover, the economy and Palestinian agriculture were adversely affected by the building of this Wall because, in order to build it, much agricultural land were taken from their owners and many types of merchandise were not allowed to leave the city or enter it. Also the city of Bethlehem city depends on pilgrims for much of its income. So, with the small amount of pilgrimage to the city, the olive wood craftsmen and small souvenir shops were also negatively affected.

Only few Palestinians are permitted to enter Jerusalem, and if only you are denied once, you will not be allowed a second trial. The Christians citizens of Bethlehem city get permits three times a year: once in Christmas and Easter; the other is after Easter. When we usually get the permits we feel like we have a limited amount of freedom outside the open air prison that we usually live in daily. As soon as we cross the check point to Jerusalem we feel that we're in a totally different world! How can that be possible if it is the same country? Most of the best roads, shopping facilities, jobs, and services are found in the other side of the wall.

It is worth mentioning that the media controls the western public's opinion regarding the Palestinian-Israeli situation. Many articles that have appeared on the Internet demonstrate many negative and incorrect facts about Palestinians. I'm not that much into politics but there are some basic and silly information that need to be corrected. For example, many people think that we live in tents and this has been mentioned in front of me by a foreign visitor, but really, people, our houses are made from brick and cement. Also, it is not true that Palestinian women are not allowed by their fathers or husbands to work or study. Statistics that were taken in 2007 show that 6829 of the females in Bethlehem city are educated, 888 of them are employed and 1874 are students; the rest are either housewives or unemployed. Also the statement that says that women are not allowed to wear western-style clothes is totally wrong because nowadays most of the women are wearing western-style clothes; only a small part are wearing the traditional Palestinian dresses and most of the Muslims females are wearing the Jilbab, a long jacket—like dress, with a Hijab which is a scarf to cover their hair.

"Occupation, Checkpoints, Apartheid Wall, Roadblocks, Curfews, Invasion and Settlements." Do you have any idea what one of these words really means if you have never experienced it in reality? Do you know what a checkpoint is and means unless you have actually been through one? Do you know what living under occupation and to be surrounded with a Separation Wall mean unless you致e actually lived under occupation and with that wall? Of course not! Our life isn稚 easy at all; I can say on behalf of our generations that we didn稚 have a normal childhood like any other child living in any country in the world. Nor did we live in peace, throughout our life and until this moment we have lived under invasions and curfews where we had to stay at home for many hours—even for days without going out of the house out of fear of being shot if you致 e been spotted. We have suffered from the roadblocks that separate the Palestinian towns and cities from one another. Checkpoints are the most humiliating process that anyone could ever go through, while the Apartheid Wall (Separation Wall) is dividing every aspect of Palestinian life. Already many people experienced the loss of land, water, and resources which provide them with a daily income. Palestinian villages and towns near the Wall have become isolated ghettos where movement in and out is limited, if not impossible.

This is our LIFE!
This is REALITY!
So is PEACE out of reach?

Sandra Ma'ayeh

Our Bethlehem

Bethlehem is the most beautiful city in the world. Sure it is, everyone's place of birth and holds a very special place in one's heart. It means so much to be born in the same place as our Lord Jesus Christ Himself was born in. For me, our life is just very simple and usual; I'm living my everyday life, doing what I have to do, studying, dreaming, and planning for the future; but to others, my life could be considered as complete madness.

We are living in an open-heaven cage, a roofless prison. For us, this situation will, some day, be over; for others, this situation is helpless and unbearable. But let me tell you about My Bethlehem.

I happen to live just facing the Nativity church. It is quite an experience to hear the bells that are rung in Bethlehem every day.

I always heard my grandmother say that her grandparents always told her "Bethlehem is surrounded by Evil and Danger, but never gets to see them." But this proved to be wrong when the siege on the Nativity church took place in 2001. The church and the Manger square were just a big TV screen, live, 3-D broadcast. I was an 11-years old girl at that time, and my uncle's family had come to sleep over in our house that night because it was Easter, and our family tradition is to have a very nice breakfast in the morning, but we ended up two families trapped in a basement under the house, praying the rosary most of the time so that peace might come over Bethlehem and Palestine.

I remember it all as if it was yesterday. All the fear, just hearing the houses being torn down, knowing so well that they are next to our house, waking up in the middle of the night at the sound of people screaming, then seeing my cousins getting themselves ready to go out in the cold weather if the soldiers chose our house by hazard and shouted in broken Arabic: (Eftakh Bab!) which means: (Open the door!). Human beings surely adapt with the surrounding area. Yes we got so adapted to the sound of the bullets, the trembling of our house building, if a tank chose to decorate the pavement and the street with its trail, and hearing the houses being demolished; our only concern was to pray that no one got killed in the harsh procedure. It didn't matter if you were sick or not, needed medication or not, you just had to endure, for the love of our Bethlehem.

Many, many sorrows, your heart can be filled with, but you cannot rewrite them in few words. You experience despair, loneliness to know that you are alone in this world—as a country, and that death could come at any time. A close friend of mine, our class's Angel, our Christine Saadeh, was murdered by the Israeli soldiers; of course, they gave their overall heartbreaking-reason, she was killed by mistake! Oh, like thousands others; by mistake . . . Our Angel was killed in 2003, my friends and I just didn't believe this at first, we all said: 'we have a mathematics exam tomorrow, she wouldn't be out, she would be studying like the rest of us.' The right name was shown on the local TV breaking news, but she was so little that they said she was 8 years old, at that time, we were sure that it was another girl, not our class's Angel who was 12 years old. But the truth was that she was out with her parents, with the mathematics book in her hands, cars were mixed up, wrong place, wrong timing, soldiers started shooting at the family's car. Christine got scared, or maybe just courageous enough to protect her father in front of her, saving his life. The next day, we didn't have school, nor a mathematics exam; we just had a funeral.

Then why do we call her our Angel? Everyone in my class feels in a way or another that she's watching over us, like she always had when she was still among us. Christine was the goodhearted, kind and loving person that we all felt free to go and talk to; her smile was always up on her face making us all happy. We carried Christine with us in each class; we had a little place in each room we were at for her picture that we always decorated with flowers. After graduating from school, we all carried her in our hearts. For me and my friends, it was never over; we wrote her some songs that we were lucky enough to go and sing in France, in cooperation with a French singer. We sent out our voice calling for justice, peace, and safe home of our own. We all know that none of us would have been the way we are now if our Christine had not played a role to change us for the best. We know and see every day that Christine is one of hundreds of children who were murdered by the Israeli military.

Just up until 2008, that our Bethlehem was revived again with tourists and pilgrimages, but still, many of the Bethlehemites suffer from being poor and unemployed, especially since the construction of the Separation Wall, where most of the workers that used to labor in Jerusalem lost their jobs due to lack of permission to pass the borders within our own home—checkpoints. In the good old days, as my father says, they used to go wherever they wanted, they'd just ride the car and go to the sea, to Nazareth, anywhere they wished for, with no borders. But this seems like a nice dream for me. Since I was born, there has an increase of violence and conflicts, if not in Bethlehem, our the cities of the West Bank, then in our Gaza. The 20 minutes that used to take my parents to go by car to Jerusalem now takes me one hour at least, because of the great checking point at the northern entrance of Bethlehem city; all of the high-sensor machines, the yelling soldiers behind the thick windows, and the violations of the human rights for one at least to be able to travel in one's country freely with no boundaries. The same strategy is used against us when we wish to travel abroad, since we have no open airport of our own, we are obliged to travel through Jordan.

In my Bethlehem City, I'm living my everyday life as simple as could be, giving out to others as I have learned from my family and neighbors. I'm a native Palestinian Catholic, doing what I have to do, to be able to love my enemy as much as I love myself, therefore to live my Bible. I'm studying and looking forward to finishing my studies and getting my degree because I believe that I can raise my country by hard work, and dreaming because no one has a hold on my dreams if I dare to dream of having a home of my own, the same exact one that had been stolen from me in 1948, then of which I was accused of being a terrorist, just for trying to protect what's ours. I am planning for my future; I am optimistic as I learned to be from people around me, even though we know that at anytime we might die, our country might cease to exist, or the violence and the occupation just might go away. We just ask the world to pray with us for peace, and for us for patience.

By Mary Mousallam

Palestinian Tradition and Israeli Permission

As a small Palestinian family living in a humble house in the Old City of Jerusalem trying to make life look more beautiful through studying and having the highest degrees, my elder sister who graduated from Bethlehem University with a Bachelor's degree in Chemistry went to Birzeit University to for a Masters Degree in Environmental Water, where, after passing one semester successfully there, she surprised us by telling us that she met her soul mate, someone from Birzeit. (Birzeit means "Well of Olive Oil" referring to the wells in which its inhabitants historically stored virgin-pressed olive oil. It is a small 14 km2 town on the outskirts of <u>Ramallah</u> in the central part of the <u>West Bank</u>).

We were so happy for her, but as traditions and habits in our country dictate, the bridegroom must come to the bride's house with his family and visit them to get to know the bride's family. As well the bride's father and brother ask about the history of the guy, his morals and the reputation of his family from people that know him and are familiar with his family.

So the guy came with his mother and sister and his eldest brother;we learned that his father had passed away four years ago. We had a great evening together as if we had know that family for a long time.

My sister continued her education at Birzeit University and continued going out with him to the local restaurants and coffee shops in Ramallah in addition to having lunch at their home or at ours. Every time she used to go out with him she came back home very happy and interested of the way they live in Birzeit and the kindness of its people. We were so happy for her being happy and choosing her life partner.

After they made their final decision that they were ready to get engaged we followed an interesting tradition that it is common in all parts of Palestine which is the asking for my sisters hand (when the man propose to the lady). So the bridegroom came to our house with his family, but this time with his extended family—uncles and all the old people—to propose to her officially, an event in which the bridegroom comes with bunches of flowers and a present for the bride. The eldest member of his family asked for her hand and the eldest member from our family was required to respond to their proposal positively or negatively for my sister; we gave a positive answer since both of them saw their life together.

In the past the mother of the man who wants to marry asks for good girls and visits her family to see the girl if is beautiful or not, and to check her, her family and their reputation. If everything is fine then late at night when her husband comes back from work she would tell him that she has made a visit to that family and we that they have to ask for the specific girl's hand. If the father agrees then all the men go to the bride's house and ask for her hand. After discussion, and asking about the man, the family responds to the proposal. The tradition still does exist but in a different way since life and lifestyles have changed allowing men and women to interact in their daily lives where they can see each other.

After this occasion, they commit themselves to each other, so they cannot propose to other person unless they have changed their minds and decided to break up. Usually after this, they don't wait long to get engaged. My sister and the bridegroom began to search for a hall and arrange for the engagement party and other details, like a dress for the bride and a suit for the bridegroom. They bought everything they needed, found a big nice hall in Ramallah, decorated it in flowers and invited their family and friends. At that day, as per custom, the people went to the hall and wait for the couples to enter, who after going to the studio to get some photos for memories, came to the party hall where the people were waiting for them. They entered like a queen and a king through the people clapping for them with the soft music playing, inviting people to dance and share with them their happiness, and to spend with them this lovely night—the formation of a mall Christian family.

Usually in Palestine, they stay a year or so engaged and after that they get married as was the case for my sister. That year was really very busy for them and passed so fast for them and for us. The bridegroom, who had just finished building the house, was busy with other work, including painting, finishing off the kitchen, and decorating it with staff. So they were patiently seeing it being finished part by part. They also were filling their days by going out with friends and family, as well celebrating Christmas, New Year, and Easter. Easter has a special tradition in which the bridegroom's family makes us a visit and brings one hundred one pieces of sweets and one hundred eggs. The 100 pieces are for the family and the piece is for the bride. However, in Jerusalem we don't have such tradition and, although we did not want to accept them they insisted and I must admit that it was really such an interesting tradition!

After they had their house painted and was ready they looked for furniture and decoration staff. Now we come to the interesting part of their tradition which is the wedding arrangement and tradition (that each culture has in its own interesting way to suit its lifestyle). It was really interesting for us experiencing these traditions since they are completely different than ours in Jerusalem where we are living, and we had experienced weddings only in our area.

Three days before the wedding date, they have a celebration that is called "Henna party." On this day the groom's family comes to our house with the women wearing the traditional Palestinian costumes singing traditional songs and holding the henna in a plate decorated by flowers. They enter the house where my sister and her friends and family welcome them and after dancing a bit they put some of the henna on her hand and on her foot and as well on the hands of other girls watching there. After they are done and have some sweets and drink their coffee they invite all the people there to their house. So after they left we prepared ourselves to go to their house at Birzeit, and took with us suitcases of my sister's clothes to her new home which is on the floor above the bridegroom's family to which we were all invited. All of the guests are encouraged to see their future house, and have some food and drinks. This tradition is an extended old tradition where the bridegroom did not see his bride till the day of the wedding day as I have mentioned Although, the groom saw her with his mother when they asked for her hand, we maintain the tradition of not changing the bride for one of her sisters, by having her marked by dye as witnessed by the other girls. So nowadays we still use this tradition just for the purpose of not losing it and not for the purpose of marking my sister since he has already seen her and knows her very well.

They had rest after a very long night with dancing, dreaming of their wedding day, their big day. After three days their big day came, so my sister went to the hair dresser and wore her nice white dress and went to her home and waited for his family to come and take her. At the same time the bridegroom stayed at home where all his friends and family members came with the barber and gave him a haircut, and they served an alcoholic Palestinian drink called arak or anise and no other kind of drink.

Then, on the shoulders of his friends, brothers, and cousins, he was taken the church singing traditional Palestinian songs and waving decorated sticks and the Palestinian scarves. At the door of the church he waited for her with the priest. In the mean time we arrived at the church with the bride and her maid of honor in their decorated car with flowers. My father and I ushered her out of the car, took her hand and gave her to the priest at the door of the church. He took her her hand and entered the church, and said Mass. Then the bride and the bridegroom with their parents and very close families go to their home to put dough at the front door of their future home. This means that their home will be fruitful just like it is, and they eat a piece of bread and water with sugar for their life to be sweet just like that water. Later they went to the studio to take some photos. And then all people were invited to a reception where food and drinks of all kind are served and people danced with the bride and bridegroom. At almost the end of the party the bride and all the female friends just left the party stage and gathered with candles in their hands and then came back to the stage and started dancing alone with the candles in their hands while all the men on stage dance the Palestinian folk dance, known the "dabkeh."

We celebrated and shared with them every moment of their happiness but being under occupation and the situation we are living in doesn't make our happiness at its best since we were worried about her future from the political way of view since she used to live in Jerusalem which is under the Israeli authority and she has a Jerusalemite ID that we call the blue ID while her husband is living in Birzeit which is in the West Bank under the Palestinian authority and he has Palestinian ID that we call the green ID. The difference among them is that the one holding the blue ID(Israeli ID) can travel to the West Bank and other places easily in addition to other health facilities while the ones holding the Green ID (Palestinian) can travel within the West Bank only, unless they get permission from Israel to enter Jerusalem and other parts under the Israeli authority but they rarely get such permissions. When all the family members apply for the permission sometimes they all get it and sometimes not all of them. Under the Israeli law it is forbidden for the ones holding the Blue ID to live in any parts of the West Bank area under any condition, and if known to be living in the West Bank they take out the ID from them and leave them without any benefits and at the same time the Palestinian authority doesn't issue any IDs or passports. There is a possibility that my sister can issue a blue ID card for him, but the procedures may take years and they need proof and so many papers. So for my sister she is living in the unknown. In the future if she may have an occasion in Jerusalem she would probably not go or she may go without her husband since he doesn't have a permission. Writing about that subject it may raise questions to you about how they used to visit us; well, we moved to our house at Al-Ram which is very near Ramallah and located in the West Bank which we had abandoned out of fear of losing our IDs as well as work and educational opportunities that we have in Jerusalem in the Old City. So by this way my sister's husband and his family could visit us easily and with no need for permission which, if they waited for, may have resulted in a delayed wedding or no wedding at all.

Elias Kattou'a

A Movie called Palestine

Palestine in movies . . . We all watch movies, and there are some times when we feel as if we were part of this movie. People mostly feel the characters' happiness and sorrows, sometimes you experience joy when you see a happy ending of a movie, while some other times you will shed tears when you see a very sad ending. These movies are a modern way of telling the stories, and I'm thankful to the 3D technology nowadays, because you are often able to watch the movie as if you were inside this movie. But what will be your feeling if you are in one of these movies for real? Well, we in Palestine are in a very big movie. A movie that has been played for the last 62 years and all the world is watching this movie, but the thing is that this movie is shown to most of the viewers from one perspective and so it's a very special movie; just imagine if you are seeing a movie and for some reason half of the scenes are missing . . . Logically, in that case, you will not understand the idea of the movie, you will be missing its parts. That's the case in the Palestinian movie; mostly all the viewers from around the world are missing the most important part of it.

Palestine is a law abiding country. "A Law Abiding Citizen" is a movie I've seen recently that talks about a father whose wife and young daughter were murdered in front of his eyes by two thugs, and due to the corrupted court system the killers were given minor sentences. The one who killed the two victims was sentenced in jail for 5 years, and the one who cooperated was sentenced to death after ten years. But having a powerful enough motive, the main character in the movie—the father—started to plan revenge. Ten years later the person who lost everything and hence capable of anything starts to take his own revenge towards those who caused him a very big loss. Starting with the killers ending up with the whole corrupted system of judges, in a very smart, elegant, and complicated way he murdered them. As human beings we all hate killings, we all hate crimes and we all love to live in peace and happiness, but on the other hand we can see that we are supporting the main character in his vengeance; why do you think so? Is it because we like to see someone killed?! For sure that's not the case; it's because we humans hate unfairness, we all love justice, also we can't understand the bad people and we wish they stop their evil acts for good. Some might argue about the way we can bring bad people into the good acts, but most will agree that something has to be done and that these bad people must be punished for their bad behaviors, in order to bring back law and order.

Anyway back to the law abiding citizen—in the movie I loved it when the main character took revenge of those who raped his wife and killed her along with his only 6 years old daughter, and again its not that I loved to see blood and it's not that I loved the way the father used violence against others because there are other ways in which law can get the ones lost right. Also it's not that I am a terrorist, it's that I am a human being who loves justice which we can achieve in different ways. After all what I said I want you now to imagine watching this movie with some of the lost scenes which were cut! Especially that the removed scenes are the most important ones. For example imagine that the scene of the wife and the daughter being killed right in front of the father has been removed, and every other scene that explains the actions of fury and revenge the father did, just imagine watching the scenes of the father going around the city killing people for no reason; at this point let's see what is the difference? What will be your feelings while watching the movie? In the first case when you watched the full movie, you will mostly feel sympathy toward the main character and you will feel satisfaction when you see him getting his rights back by punishing the bad guys—though I don't agree with him using violence. Now try to compare these feelings with those that you felt while watching the movie without the removed scenes. Well, you will be probably waiting for a hero or a police to come and arrest this serial killer and submit him to trials, so that you can get a good ending! Can you notice how things can change when the critical scenes are deleted! The story won't be complete and will be, for sure, misunderstood. Unfortunately those scenes removed from this movie are almost like the Palestinian movie, which is viewed in many parts of the world, specially in Europe and the United States in which Palestine is not understood correctly.

Palestine is Pandora in the movie, "Avatar," which I'm sure some of you watched. For the first time, we, the audience of the movie wanted the Na'vis to win! Again its not because we love aliens and hate humans. It's because, here, humans are acting in an evil way and the aliens are acting in a very peaceful way; they're a nation which wants to be left alone in peace. Again we are on the just side even though it's not the human side; why is that? Naturally, it's because we human being love justice, and now, assuming that most of us have watched the movie, "Avatar," I invite you to play the game of removing scenes—cut them in your mind. Let's cut the scene of the Pandora in the homeland of the Na'vi's, in which to them, we, the humans, are the aliens. Let's cut any scenes that show that the humans are the ones who want war, let's cut any scene that shows that the aliens are a life loving creatures who are at one with their surrounding nature. Let's only show the scenes of these creatures screaming and killing humans, and, why not delete the scene where the main character says, "And that this . . . this is our land!" Let's just imagine what would be the difference in both cases. In this version you will hate the guts of these blue aliens, and you will call the main character a traitor! And you will wait impatiently for all the aliens to be eliminated in a way or another, in order to have the good ending you're looking for. In other words it's just another bad alien vs. good humans movie; on the other hand, in the original movie many people lost it as they saw the main character saying, "This is our land!" At that moment we probably wanted to fight against humans with the aliens. That is because we got emotionally attached to the story, especially when we felt that the aliens were defending their homeland, and to a certain point, we forgot that these blue creatures are aliens, because in that case the human were the outlanders and the occupiers. Because we believe in justice, we wanted them to win and we were happy when they did, and no one will ever say that the movie had a sad ending because the humans lost the battle! Well, now the world is seeing a different Avatar movie! By viewing the Palestine film, not knowing that Palestine is just another Pandora, and it is the homeland of the Na'vis—"Palestinians"—and the humans in this real movie are Israelis. But do you know what? This movie has been cut!! I mean the scene when the aliens said, "this is our land" were removed.

Now let's go to the movie, "Palestine," around the world; let's see what the majority of westerners think of the Palestinian people. First that they are giving the poor Israeli people some bad times, second that they are savage people who don't know anything but killing and they hate peace, that's why they are considered to be a danger to the Israeli security. These people have came out of nowhere to bother Israel! Well here are some of the scenes that have been cut.

The scene that shows that Palestine has been the HOMELAND of the Palestinians for more than 1500 years, the scene that shows that Palestine was just a peaceful country full of good people, just before the Balfour promise of making it a homeland for the Jews in 1917, where the people of Palestine were living in peace and harmony for hundreds of years before the Israelis occupied the land;the scene that shows that Palestine used to be free just like your countries; the scene where the Israeli forces came to occupy Palestine by killing the Palestinian people in mass barbaric murders; the scene where more than 4.000,000 Palestinian people were forced to flee, leaving their homeland and properties behind just to stay alive, running away from the black Israeli waves of death; the scene where every Jewish person from every country around the world is urged to stay in Palestine and some are paid to do so just to increase the numbers of the Israelis. I mean, do you know that just 62 years earlier there was no country called Israel, there was only Palestine, the Home land of Palestinians who tried to fight in order to get their full rights, fighting against the killing of the thousands of the Palestinians, which makes Israel a country built on the blood of others. Moreover, where did all these Israeli settlers came from? They all have other citizenships, they were all born somewhere else.

These scenes are all removed; without them the world looks at Palestinians as terrorists, and Israelis are the heroes. The scenes that made the victims look as if they were criminals, and of course you will never see a scene of an Israeli soldier killing a parent while holding his young child between his bare arms, or an Israeli rocket killing a 2 months old girl, or Israeli soldiers using tanks and the F-16 striking Palestinian homes. And, yes, you always see the Israeli people who were mildly injured or just having break downs on TV, but you never see the scenes where the small legless or handless or eyeless Palestinian kids are crying for losing their whole family under Apache missiles.

We Palestinians are law abiding citizens who want to live safely in our Pandora . . . so please check for the removed scenes before watching our movie, so that you can have a clearer idea about what is going on, because we are a nation that wants to live in its own country, on its lands, with peace, love and harmony.

Fadi Masshour

Palestinians Daily Life

When I was asked to write this paper about Palestine, I faced difficulties in choosing the subject I want to focus on since the Palestinian cause has very long history, and endless issues to be raised and discussed. Describing the Palestinian cause is much different than seeing it on the ground. However, in my paper I will try my best to draw a small picture of Palestinians daily life. I will focus on how Palestinians live in different conditions because they hold different ID cards according to the areas they live in. I will make it clear in my paper that Palestine is not a State next to Israel, and Palestine is not a country close to Pakistan. I totally understand the confusion which the internationals have regarding the Palestinian—Israeli conflict, but I feel that if I had never existed when I tell internationals that I am from Palestine and many of them think that it is Pakistan or a place near Israel.

First of all, let's start with a small introduction about Palestine. When the Zionist movement was founded and became a formal organization in 1897, the Zionists decided to establish a Jewish State, which is what they call now Israel, in Palestine. As a first step to achieve this goal, Jews from Europe started to immigrate in 1882 and settle down in Palestine. The first Jewish settlement was created in Palestine in 1882. Zionist movement continued strengthening itself and lobbying its goal of establishing a Jewish State on the lands of Palestine among European governments, especially the British government. At that time, Britain had interests in Palestine, and so the British government's interests met with the Zionist movement's interests in Palestine. Accordingly, in 1917, the British government adopted the Zionists' aim of founding a Jewish State in Palestine through the Balfour Declaration in which the British government promised to give land to Jews to establish their State. This resulted in increasing the Jewish immigration to Palestine. Consequently, Jews formed 7% of the total Palestinian population and owned 2% of the Palestinian land during World War I.

Many Zionist and Jewish agencies were established outside Palestine and later on in Palestine to prepare for the creation of the Jewish State. The British Mandate, which started in Palestine in 1920, helped the Zionist movement to found different agencies like "The Jewish Agency for Palestine", which represented Jewish interests in Palestine and promoted Jewish immigration. During the British Mandate of Palestine (1920-1948), the Zionist movement became financially, institutionally and military strong enough to establish the Jewish State on the Palestinian lands. In 1947, the United Nations General Assembly issued the Partition Plan (Resolution 181), which recommended the establishment of the Jewish and Arab States in Palestine and the internationalism of the Jerusalem area. This resolution recommended the establishment of the Jewish State on 55% of the Palestinian land. Later on, in 1948, the Zionist movement announced the establishment of the Jewish State, Israel, and the British government announced the end of the British Mandate on Palestine.

Arabs in Palestine realized the danger of the Zionist movement on Palestine before Balfour Declaration, and they became more aware of that danger after Balfour Declaration. They tried to resist it, but Palestinians at that time were simple farmers and didn't have power compared to European and Zionist powers. All their efforts failed.

In 1948, Israelis committed ethnic cleansing against Palestinians. They used a well planned Zionist strategy to kill and expel hundreds of thousands of Palestinians from their homes and villages. Around 80% of the total Palestinian population was expelled. More than 530 Palestinian villages were depopulated and completely destroyed. The 1948 Ethnic Cleansing resulted in having Palestinian refugees in Syria, Lebanon and Jordan, and refugees inside Palestine in the West Bank and Gaza Strip. Around 6 million Palestinian refugees are in Syria, Jordan and Lebanon and are prevented by Israel from returning to Palestine despite the fact that the UN General

Assembly recognized in 1948 the right of Palestinian refugees to return. Furthermore, the 1948 Ethnic Cleansing resulted in the Israeli occupation of 78% of the Palestinian land. 1948 is a critical year for the Palestinians because it was the beginning of dividing the Palestinians into different areas. In 1967, Israel occupied the rest of Palestine. Therefore, the Security Council established "Resolution 242" recommending the Israeli withdrawn to 1967 borders.

The Palestinian cause has a very long history and issues to be raised. This paper won't be enough at all to tackle all the Palestinian—Israeli conflict. However, I would like to make it clear that well planned Israeli policies practiced against the Palestinians resulted in dividing the Palestinians according to areas; Palestinian refugees in Lebanon, Syria and Jordan; Palestinians of the West Bank; Palestinians of the Gaza Strip; Palestinians of Jerusalem; and Palestinians of 1948 lands. In my paper, I will focus on the Palestinians of the West Bank, and Jerusalem. This division has created deep difficulties and obstacles in their daily life.

Palestinians living in the West Bank are Palestinian ID card holders. Although the West Bank is considered to be under the control of the Palestinian Authority, it is under the occupation of Israel but in t means other than direct occupation. There are more than 528 permanent and temporary checkpoints and physical roadblocks created by the Israeli government among all West Bank cities, villages and towns. In any moment, Israel blocks these checkpoints and prevents Palestinians from traveling from one place to another. Palestinians, who have to travel every day to work in another city or town, have to pass through at least one checkpoint. Israeli soldiers on these checkpoints check the Palestinians' ID cards, cars and taxis before they allow them to pass to be able to go to another city. Every morning, Israeli soldiers let cars and taxis pass through these checkpoints slowly in order to humiliate the Palestinians and make them wait in a long queue, and so make them late to their jobs and work. So a Palestinian has to get worried every morning and calculate when he should leave the house to be able to reach his work on time hopefully. Imagine then if a group of university students, girls and boys, decide to go for a trip to another city in the West Bank. They will spend most of the trip on checkpoints being checked and humiliated.

I want to tell you a small story about a trip I had with my university. In September 2006, Bethlehem University arranged an educational visit to the Arab American University in Jenin, a city in the north of the West Bank, about 100km from Bethlehem. I was so excited about this educational visit, for it was the first time I'd have the chance to go to Jenin. As a Palestinian trapped inside the separation wall surrounding Bethlehem, it is rare that I get to travel anywhere to other West Bank cities. At 7am we left Bethlehem by bus and headed for Jenin. Shortly after leaving, we faced the first checkpoint, called "The Container", which is in Wad Annar, about 30 minutes from Bethlehem. Israeli soldiers, who were at the Container, stopped our bus and two of them entered it and, one-by-one, began checking our Palestinian ID cards. One of these two soldiers loudly read one of our Palestinian student's names: Nakhlah, from his ID card. Nakhlah means a palm tree. The Israeli soldier started laughing when he read the student's name, Nakhlah, and he started making fun of his name by saying, "You Nakhlah, let me see if you are as tall as Nakhlah. Is that your real name? Or you are just kidding me! Come on tell me you fool, stupid Nakhlah. You are a fool and stupid as a Nakhlah tree, right? Tell me, where are you going, stupid Nakhlah tree? I will not let you go until you tell me that you are a fool as a Nakhlah tree, and tell me where you are going." Both Israeli soldiers took our Palestinian ID cards and began yelling at us, "Come on, all of you get out of the bus. Wait for us on the side of the road until we return your ID cards and allow you to get back on the bus." They prevented us from sitting down or moving. So, we had no choice other than to stand, waiting for them to return our ID cards, and sweating under the hot sun. One hour later, one of our group members volunteered to go to the soldier to ask about our ID cards. When the soldier saw the student walking toward him, he went crazy and started shouting, ordered him to go back, and aimed his gun at him. The student was forced to return back to us. Two hours later, the Israeli soldiers finally returned our ID cards, and allowed us to enter the bus and continue our journey to Jenin. We were so exhausted and thirsty. Our legs and backs hurt from standing so long. What happened to us felt like torture. In many ways, I believe, under international law, being forced to stand in the hot sun at gunpoint for three hours would constitute torture.

A few kilometers from the Container we picked up the rest of our group—holders of Jerusalem ID cards—who were waiting for us on the side of the road. Palestinians with Jerusalem ID cards are not allowed to pass through the Container to get to other parts of the West Bank, such as Jenin. They must travel through Jerusalem, which means any group leaving from Bethlehem to travel to the north parts of the West Bank usually has to separate for segments of the trip, making any excursion even more time-consuming. This Israeli policy seems to be used to separate Palestinians—holders of Palestinian ID cards and the holders of Jerusalem ID cards—from one another, and to make their lives harder and more frustrating. However, we didn't surrender to these cruel and inhumane policies. Instead, we asked those students who were holders of Jerusalem ID cards to wait for us a few kilometers after the Container and then we met up with them so we could go to Jenin as one united Palestinian group. Our enjoyment lasted for one hour before it was interrupted by the second checkpoint, Zaatarah, about 80km from the Container checkpoint. Our bus driver was ordered to park on the side of the road by Israeli soldiers at Zaatarah checkpoint. Two soldiers entered the bus and began shouting at us, forcing us, once again, to get out of the bus. They made us stand in one line close to the bus. One of them took our ID cards, and counted them. Another counted us to make sure that there were as many of us as there were ID cards. A third soldier checked our ID cards one-by-one on his computer to make sure that none of us was a "terrorist". The soldiers made us stand still in one queue outside the bus for an hour, preventing us from making any movement or even sitting down to rest. After taking an hour to check our ID cards, they finally permitted us to go back to our bus and continue our long trip to Jenin. Finally, at 2pm, we reached Jenin. A 100km journey took us seven hours. We were stopped by Israeli soldiers at three checkpoints on the short distance to Jenin. So, can you imagine how Palestinians can spend their weekends?

The Separation Wall that was built around the West Bank divided the Palestinians more. Jerusalem, 1948 and 1967 lands are inside the Separation Wall. The West Bank is outside the Separation Wall. Palestinians living in the West Bank and holding Palestinian ID cards are not allowed at all to enter Jerusalem, 1948 and 1967 lands.

They are allowed to move only inside the West Bank. So, relatives and friends who live in both sides can't see or visit each other. When Palestinians from the West Bank want to travel abroad, they have to travel through Jordan to their headed destination despite the fact that there is an airport inside the Separation Wall. Palestinians even have to get a visa to every country they intend to go to. Palestinians don't get visas at airports. Instead, they have to apply an application for a visa to an embassy, and wait for weeks until they receive an approval of getting a visa.

Do you know that a Palestinian from Jerusalem cannot get married to a Palestinian from the West Bank because he/ she will lose his/ her rights in Jerusalem in addition to the big probability of losing his/ her Jerusalem ID card? So, Palestinians from the West Bank and Jerusalem have to ask each other first what kind of ID cards they hold before they decide to get married or even fall in love.

Jerusalemites are Israeli ID card holders for residency only. They are not considered to be Israeli citizens as Palestinians of 1948 lands. Jerusalemites are not treated equally as Israelis in Jerusalem. They have to pay higher taxes. They wait in long queues for long hours under the sun and rain if they need to get formal documents from official and governmental Israeli offices. They don't have job opportunities inside Jerusalem. They are not allowed to work or live in the West Bank. If the Israeli government finds out that some Jerusalemites are living in the West Bank, they take their ID cards, expel them from Jerusalem and deprive them of their rights. Jerusalemites, who are working in the West Bank, are considered to be working illegally according to the Israeli laws, and they are under the danger of losing their rights and ID cards. So, what can Jerusalemites do in this case to live a proper life? They have no job opportunities in Jerusalem, they cannot leave Jerusalem to live in the West Bank, and they are considered by the Israeli government illegal people if they work in the West Bank.

Living in Jerusalem is expensive for Jerusalemites as they don't earn enough money. Besides the high taxes Jerusalemites have to pay, rents of houses are very high. Therefore, many Jerusalemites live in small and unhealthy houses. They even cannot get a license for building a small house easily. They need to go through long procedures for years and pay hundreds of thousands of Shekels (Israeli currency) until they receive a license for building small houses with limited sizes specified by the Israeli government.

Jerusalemites face serious problems with the Israeli government like house demolition, arrestment, lack of services they receive from the Israeli government although they pay high taxes, and they have bad infrastructure in their neighborhoods. Besides that, Jerusalemites who get another nationality from another country lose their Jerusalem ID cards and are not considered to be Palestinians or Jerusalemites any more. They are considered foreigners, and they need to get an entry visa for three months from Israel every time they want to enter Israel. Many Jerusalemites holding another nationality and living abroad are denied entering Israel. The Israeli government is using all means, policies and laws to force Jerusalemites to leave Jerusalem.

The conditions the Palestinians live in the different areas—the West Bank, Jerusalem, Gaza Strip, 1948 lands—are becoming worse day by day. I would like note here that the aim of Zionism is establishing a State for Jews only, and this doesn't match the principles of democracy which Israel claims to have. So, Israel will use all means and policies against Palestinians everywhere to achieve this goal. Palestinians living anywhere have no clear identity like Palestinians living in 1948 lands. They are Israeli ID card holders and considered to be Israeli citizens although they are the original inhabitants of that area. However, they are now minorities in 1948 lands, and they don't have the same equal rights the Israelis themselves have. Israel is using discriminatory policies against them in education, job opportunities, owning properties, and infrastructure of their towns. Palestinians in 1948 lands have serious problems in identifying themselves; are they Palestinians but holding Israeli ID cards? Are they Israelis but having no equal rights as Israelis? Are they Arabs-Israelis? Are they Palestinians-Israelis? In addition, Palestinians in the Gaza Strip have different life conditions and circumstances. Gaza Strip is totally separated from Israel, the West Bank, and the whole world. Palestinians in the West Bank and Israel cannot at all go to the Gaza Strip. Palestinians living in Gaza are not allowed to leave to somewhere else neither to West Bank nor to abroad.

I wish, my dear readers, that I have succeeded, through this paper, in describing a small side of the Palestinians life, and that I have succeeded in making it clear that so-called Israel is what we call Palestine.

By Ronza Al-Madbouh

A Punishment of a Prisoner

The story which I am writing is a true story based on sad facts. It is a reality due to the Israeli occupation of occupied Palestinian territories; sadly my story is about a Palestinian citizen called Fayez, who was born in the year 1961 in the town of Bani Na'im east of Hebron. He is married and has eight daughters and seven sons.

His story began four years ago, when Fayez was arrested by the Israeli soldiers on 15th February, 2006, after being chased by them for 6 years. After spending two years in an Israeli prison, Fayez started complaining about having severe pain in his body.

When he was checked by the prison doctor, he told the doctor about his pain, so the prisoner doctor examined him. He told him that he didn't have any illnesses, diseases or health issues. While each time he paid a visit to the doctor in the prison, and told him about this non stoppable pain, he would hear the same answer, and was mocked by the doctor and told that it's all about his fantasy.

In his third year in the prison, Fayez discovered that he had a terminal illness and was suffering from cancer, but he also discovered that the disease had already spread throughout his body, especially in the pancreas and liver, while some other organs in his body had been severely harmed by this disease.

He asked to leave the prison for the sake of treatment and therapies in a hospital, but the Israeli authorities refused to release him to go for cancer therapy treatment. Moreover, when his family visited him in the prison, or the prison hospital (clinic), they were subjected to humiliation, harassment, and were prevented from visiting him up to the end.

The Palestinian Prisoner's Society began a campaign in the year 2009 to help release Fayez from the prison in order to save his life, and after some time, the Society finally succeeded in bringing him freedom, hoping to bring him a cure as well. But after four years of battling his disease in the prison, and not being able to get medical treatment, the cancer was in its very last stages and had reached a place of no hope. Fayez died on 1st May 2010 because of cancer; though he was released from the prison, the doctors could not save his life, due to lack of medication and medical care offered to him at his early stages, and it is well known that cancer patients might live better if their disease is diagnosed in its early stages. But after the spread of cancer in his body, his case was no longer curable. The doctors said that if the disease was detected, and Fayez was released from the prison earlier, they would have been able to give him good medical care that would have helped him fight his illness.

Fayez's family said that the medical neglect of the doctors in the prison made Fayez suffer and was the only thing that made his cancer get worse. And they also said that Fayez was complaining about the food served in the prison because it was bad and not edible; also he complained about the bad environment of the prison and the lack of good services offered.

Finally, there are more than 11.000 Palestinian prisoners in the Israeli prisons. They are all suffering the way Fayez and many of his previous mates did. Some other Palestinian prisoners, like Murad, who is 27 year old and had cancer in his eyes, died in 2009 after spending three years in the occupation prisons.

Unfortunately, this is a very brief story about the life of one Palestinian prisoner among others who are kids, youngsters, women and men, struggling to find a better life in the prisons and are fighting the days to pass quickly so that they can get their freedom, and live in peace among their family members.

By: Ahmad Issa Motira

Sara

I'll always remember that day
And it'll never be forgot
It was the 5th of May
When Sara was shot

We were playing down the street
And suddenly fog filled the entire place
I told Sara let's go home
Sara refused, she was full of grace

I was scared, I ran home
I shouted, Sara come they're coming
Sara stared and said, I AM home
I cried but Sara was still there—standing-

Afraid of going home alone, I looked at her from a distance
I felt guilty for leaving her, so I decided to go
Walking with slow footsteps and fast beating heart
I heard them near but I wanted to be there for her

I screamed, Sara I'm here. She turned to see me
I saw a shadow right behind her
And then
Sara was shot in front of my eyes

I was paralyzed there.
He shouted, girl go home, you're not allowed to be here
I heard Sara's tender voice saying
This IS our HOME and I'm NOT leaving here!!
Nor will I Sara, Nor will I.

By Mays Ba'bish

Sea on the Highway!

I am a young Palestinian Christian woman in my early twenties. I was excited to receive my holiday travel permit, allowing me to visit lands occupied by the military in 1967, and Palestinian areas in Israel. Most other months of the year I am not allowed to go into Jerusalem, Jaffa, Haifa or Nazareth, because I am a Palestinian.

Mostly, Palestinian ID holders can only get permit for special cases like visiting a hospital when they are sick. Workers also get permits from their employers, via Israel, but they have to return to the West Bank before evening. As a Christian though, I get permits at Christmas, and sometimes Easter, so I can visit religious sites that I am usually barred from.

Twice! I went through the checkpoint—only twice even though the permit was for a whole month. I still had to work and life carried on, so for the 31 days of permission I only had two opportunities where I managed to pass through the checkpoint. My first time was to get to Jerusalem and visit holy sites with the scout troop I guide.

On the second day, I was going to go to the sea.

It was 10 January 2010, and it started off as a normal day. I woke up, had breakfast, watched TV, and waited for lunch. The phone rang. My aunt was on the line and said they were going to Jaffa. I thought: the sea!!

It's been some time since I've been to the sea and since I had permission I thought I should take the opportunity. I sent a message to all my friends. Some of them agreed to join me, and since we could not drive Palestinian cars into Israel, we decided to navigate the Israeli sherut system. That was the first mistake.

Off we went to the checkpoint—five young women and a teenage boy.

The Bethlehem checkpoint was crowded. Soldiers were videotaping the crowd. We stood there for more than an hour, humiliated as we were searched one-by-one on our way through the turnstiles and metal detectors.

Through the checkpoint and onto the Arab bus that goes to Damascus gate at the head of the Old City. We got off early and walked past the invisible armistice line into West Jerusalem where we met an Arab man, who was standing at the sherut lot. He told us to get on the van with an Israeli driver because it was "his turn." Off we go in the van heading to Tel Aviv, to the sea. With us, there were other passengers. A woman who spoke three languages offered to help us get from the sherut station in the city on to the sea. An Israeli man pretended he did not speak Arabic at first and acted like a philosopher.

Because of traffic we did not take Highway One. We took the settler bypass road that runs through the West Bank, but is forbidden for Palestinians to drive on. We watched our villages fly past from angles we had never seen them before. Just in case Palestinians do get on the road, there is a checkpoint where it veers west, back into Israeli territory.

We stopped at the checkpoint. When the Israeli policeman opened the van's door, he saw the youngest among us, the boy. He made him step out of the van.

My friend's brother does not speak Hebrew or English. He didn't understand what the soldier was telling him, so he was beaten. The driver refused to wait and wanted to leave without him. He went out of the van, spoke to the soldier, came back to tell us the boy was being sent back to Jerusalem. The philosopher urged the driver to leave.

The five of us refused to go on without him, and we exited the van. We stood in the highway and waited until he finished being questioned at the checkpoint.

Imagine: five young women standing on the highway, waiting. The young boy get finished after 15 minutes and reached us safely.

Since no car traveling on the bypass road has room for six, and we did not want to be separated, we started walking on the highway like in the movies. We tried to stop anyone to drive us to Tel Aviv but there was no point. I called my aunt's husband to come get us, but he said it would take him more than an hour to reach us due to the rush hour traffic.

We made the most of the enforced adventure, singing and dancing while walking through the highway. I made sure to take loads of pictures.

The plan, back at the first checkpoint, was to see the sunset over the Mediterranean as we sat on the beach. But guess what, the sunset on the highway was much more fun!

We walked for two hours until we reached a gas station.

Four-four-three is the road number. It was written on the top of the gas station. Road 443, the settler road that connects Jerusalem with Modi'in and Tel Aviv. It is under heavy security and is for Israelis only.

So at the gas station for Israelis only, we Palestinians drank some soft drinks and ate chocolates. We waited for another hour until my uncle picked us up.

By the time we arrived in Tel Aviv, it was 7:10 pm. He drove us to the train station directly to catch the last train to Jerusalem at 7:55pm, so there was no time to put our feet on the sand, or in the salt water. I guess the sea at night is not that exciting anyway.

Jenny Baboun

Semi-life in Hebron

My life story is so simple and short it can even end before it starts.

I'm living in the heart of the occupied city of Hebron—which is to the west of Palestine. I was born in 1981 in Jerusalem and because my mother, who is a Jerusalemite, wanted to deliver me in one of the hospitals of Jerusalem, hoping that one day I would be able to get the Jerusalem (Israeli, blue) ID so that I would be able to visit my family from my mother's side with her when she goes to visit them. But that was another dream that never came true and an approach that never happened . . . .

The problems started in my early childhood when we were affected badly by the Israeli occupation in the early days of the year 1987 when the Israeli army occupied a small piece of land. It didn't stop there but an army outpost was established on our play ground, the place were we used to play as kids and spend beautiful times, but we were soon denied playing football there, and deprived from our beautiful moments of joy while playing with our peers, while most of our activities in front of the house were stopped due to that, so we started playing in the streets as the rest of the Palestinians kids now do, due to the lack of the beautiful playgrounds that were destroyed, especially, in thatarea.

After that, within a year, we went to school which was in the city center. But the first Intifada "uprise" started, and whenever a kid threw a stone toward the army place the soldiers would invade the school and start shooting rubber bullets and gas tears bombs inside the school. So the teachers were forced to dismiss us earlier from school so that no one would be injured. But the soldiers aimed to stop the teaching process at school, and make it impossible to teach at that school or learn in it. That was meant to create an illiterate generation among the Palestinians, the way they did with my parents' generations.

This little outpost started to grow up until it became a small settlement, right in the middle of our neighborhood. Our movement inside our own neighborhood started to turn harder and harder, day after day until a very big catastrophe took place in Hebron, when the massacre at the Ibrahimi mosque happened, in which a Jewish settler came into the mosque and killed the people praying inside it. That turned our life upside down.

Since that day we have been punished, for the reason that innocent people have been killed while praying by the punisher. We had to live for six months under a continuous curfew and siege, because we were so close to the Israeli army post. That limited our movement to just about everywhere; we couldn't go out of our houses, and all what we were able to do was to play cards—so much so that we become professionals in these games.

We struggled to survive, and after the sixth month we woke to the sad reality to find that more than four hundred settlers took over around the old city with the help of the Israeli soldiers who closed all the streets in our area and closed the ways that lead to our neighborhood. The settlers were the only ones who were able to move freely and have access to the area, but we are not now allowed to walk on many of the streets, while some others we were not permitted to use. Also we are not allowed to drive cars, but we are forced to stop our cars one kilometer away from our houses. So we have to carry all the goods we buy from the stores to our houses by hand. We are also isolated from the other parts of the city, people are not allowed to visit us, and if they are willing to do so especially on special occasions and feasts, we have to ask the Israeli Army to issue permits so that we can enter to the old city of Hebron and visit us in our own homes, as if we are living inaprison.

All these actions make the settlers very strong and give them great power and strength. Moreover, these settlers who occupied our neighborhood are attacking us daily, and they use verbal and physical violence against us. They keep attacking our homes day and night to try to force us to leave our houses in order to kick us out through their control and the protection that they get from the Israeli soldiers who provide them security. It is well known that they are all armed—that's why almost all of our houses are covered with fences to shed some protection. Some of the Human Rights watchers and volunteers are trying to help us live there with the minimum basis of safety and security, because many of us have been injured, killed or lost our houses because of the brutality of the settlers.

It might take days and years to tell you about each of the struggle we are living in, the humiliation and fear we face every day, and the insecurity our kids are living in, but if you want to know the truth and have a clearer idea about what's going on here in my city, you should come here, visit, and witness the reality.

Fawaz Abuaisheh

Occupation is Hard

It's been eight years now since the Second Intifada (Al-Aqsa Intifada) started, very memorable for me and for every young Palestinian I guess. Missiles, tanks, machine guns shooting, Israeli soldiers with different kinds of weapons walking around the streets, killing civilians, threatening people not to leave there houses or less they'll be shot.

Palestinians got sick of violence and humiliation. They are exhausted from the settlers who are attacking them, the bulldozers which are destroying their houses, cutting the olive trees and the building of the massive separation wall! People are tired due to the searching of their cars and pockets on the checkpoints, due to hitting students with no reasons, maybe just for fun, who knows! Whatever kind of vandalism is done against my people, they always claim it under the "Security Reasons."

This all started when Ariel Sharon, the ex-prime minister of Israel, entered the Dome of the Rock with over 1,000 of his soldiers, who were walking into Al-Aqsa mosque holding their weapons, while Muslims were praying, declaring that the Temple Mount (Al-Haram Al-Sharif) would remain under an Israeli control. This disrespectful act in a holy place like this lit the torch; the torch of the Second Intifada that began on late September 2000.

It was in the early 2002 when the 44 days invasion took place. At a sudden, and under "Security Reasons," Israel called for a curfew on the whole West Bank. Hundreds of military jeeps full of soldiers driving down the streets of Bethlehem area, shouting on speakers, ordering natives to leave the streets and head to their houses and not to leave until a further notice.

As I remember, I was in the sports class, and as usual playing basketball with my classmates on the school court, when a black jeep parked in front of the school's open gate. It was so unusual and very shocking; we saw jeeps on TV not in real life. Later we heard the soldiers using the speakers shouting out loud, which was scary! I didn't understand what that was, because they were shouting in Hebrew. The teacher told us to leave the court and go into the building. In just a few seconds after that we heard a very loud explosion; they blew up the school's gate, and then left!

The curfew lasted for 44 days, all of Bethlehem city, no schools, no shops, no walking on the streets, no life. But jeeps, tanks and soldiers passing through the streets, and if Palestinians were seen, they would shoot in the air to scare them off, or simply just shoot at them!!! I was 12 years old then, every day some kids from the town, my cousins, my brothers and I would go out and play in the empty streets, just bored of staying at home, and whenever someone sees a jeep or a tank he would shout out loud to warn us, and we would start running away to seek a place to hide.

One afternoon, I went out with my older brother and some guys from the neighborhood to play soccer on the main street of Bethlehem. As usual I played with my brother's team because it's better, we started kicking the ball around having fun, while everybody was enjoying their times, that's when without any warning a jeep stopped in front of us and a soldier jumped out of the military jeep holding his M-16! Everybody left the ball and we started running because we were scared of the soldier. As I was running I heard gun shots, I followed my brother and hid with him behind a wall, terrified and trembling so hard! For a moment I thought my life was over; live bullets were passing all over my body and above my head, everybody was screaming and hiding, then I heard my brother screaming in a very heavy breath, and in a trembling voice saying: "Ahmad is down, he's been shot." I would never forget how my brother's face looked as he ran to pick up Ahmad. Two guys helped him out, the shooting stopped, but the soldier was still on the street. Ahmad's blood was all over the place and we had to get him to a hospital before we lost him. We had to drag him through the fields and through a very long way to reach the hospital. No way we could go back and use the other way where the soldiers were waiting. When we finally reached the hospital the doctors saw him and took him to the emergency room, I was standing next to my brother with tears filling my eyes and hatred in my eyes, thinking of going back home and never leaving again. The doctors left the emergency room after a while, and from the look on their faces I knew he was gone!!! Ahmad, my neighbor, was gone too soon forever.

I can never ever forget that day, neither my neighbor, whom I knew since I was little, and who was dying in front of my eyes. I was 12 years old only, never thought I would go through such a thing. It hurt me so bad to remember that day, tears fill my eyes whenever I tell that story, I hated the Israeli soldiers since then, and no one can blame me for this. This bad memory is stuck in my head and it will never be gone, for whenever I see a soldier, I remember what I have been through.

Occupation is hard, every Palestinian has a story, a lot of young Palestinians have been through the same situations and even through much worse situations; this is what every single Palestinian has to go through once in a while. Nobody likes to be under control and brutal humiliation, under so many limitations. We are forced to be live this way, and every day we live is a struggle for a better life though it has never been better. The following days seem even harder than the old ones which passed yesterday, but this is our life, and this is our case, while that was my story, may God be with us, since nobody else is!

Ward Qumsieh
20 Years Old
Bethlehem University, Accounting.

Urination in Palestine

Every single person should have the right to pee anytime. Stupid right to some, you may think, but no!!! In Palestine everything is different—even this essential right.

The trip from Bethlehem to Ramallah is 45 minutes, assuming no checkpoints and no traffic, of course. It's not the original historic way between the two cities, which used to take no more than 20 minutes. Privileged am I since I know a taxi driver who picks me up from work before the rush hour(around 4 pm), and I don't have to go all the way to the taxi station and wait for the taxi, then wait for the taxi to be filled with passengers, then start the journey—thereby saving me one hour in this whole process. I pay a little more money but it's worth it.

So my day started like any other day. I woke up around 6, got dressed, and went to Ramallah. I didn't sleep that well the night before, which caused me a huge headache which was cured by a couple of pills, but I was sleepy all the day which was handled by drinking *many* cups of coffee. Mindful that I had spent most of my time drinking coffee or in the bathroom, I was not productive at work that day, to say the least.

So the taxi picked me up and started our journey home. I'm going to use a new term here; it's called SMS which refers to "Stop Moving & you're Stuck" because in these situations you stop for 10 minutes, move for one second, then stop again for 10 minutes, then go through the whole thing again and again until you feel you want to walk all the way from Ramallah to Bethlehem. The first SMS we had was in Qalandaya; is it called Qalandya village or Qalandya Refugee camp or Qalanday terminal, or all the three—it's confusing to me. At one single small tiny point, cars coming from all over the country meet. Cars to and from Jerusalem. cars to and from Rmallah, cars to and from all over the West Bank!!! Anyway, this SMS lasted for 30 minutes (it usually takes 3 minutes). It's amazing how many theories you get in 30 minutes about the solution to this crazy traffic; every single travel companion in the taxi came up with at least two theories—my favorite being "to open a tunnel!!" As if the Israelis would allow!!

After finishing this SMS I started to sense the need for a bathroom, and I knew I would have to hold myself for another 45 minutes, tops. As I was thinking of what options I would have to end my misery if it got any worse, another SMS came on our way. At a small junction near a village called Jaba' there was a traffic jam; cars from all over the West Bank and from all over nearby illegal Israeli settlements meet in this small junction. You sense that suddenly all the cars from all over Palestine come here. This SMS lasted for 20 minutes and my misery intensified. I was unable to answer many phone calls as I wasn't focused on anything outside my own misery. Things literally started to blur. The taxi driver drove really fast but, of course, not fast enough for me. 20 minutes into this trip we were out of the bypass roads(made to connect the illegal Israeli settlements), and we reached another SMS. It's called Ma'ali Adomim Junction. Any car that wants to leave from the northern part of the West Bank to the southern part of it, should pass by this junction, not to mention the cars that leave from the illegal settlement (Ma'ali Admomim) and another one called Qidar. So this SMS—my favorite one—lasted for 30 minutes!!! We reached Al'Izareya (Bethany), which is part of the Palestinian territories but in Area C which puts it under the Israeli military control. Then came the Abu Deis Area, and after 10 minutes we faced a traffic jam caused by Israeli checkpoint, which is placed between two Palestinian Territories. To do what? I have no idea, and, although, lately I hadn't seen any traffic, this day was special for some reason, and the 17 year old soldier had to check every ID card. So this SMS was caused by hundreds of cars coming from north of the West Bank which had to pass by this checkpoint, as there's no other way. It was kind of O.K. at the beginning. Why? Because we saw the soldiers opening the cars and taking a long look at the IDs and then letting the people go. But for some reason our car was set aside, our IDs were collected, and taken somewhere. While we were waiting in the car, men started to complain because they wanted to smoke, but no complaints from me. I was thinking of going to one of the nearby houses, but we were not permitted to leave the car. Imagine me getting out of the car and running to one of the houses! The soldiers would shoot and I would die for the sake of a bathroom. What a nice cause to die for!

We were released after 40 minutes or so. By now, I had stopped calculating the time, while the rest of my journey and how I got home is a blur that I hardly remember.

This tiny misery, compared with what all the Palestinians face every day is unimportant, but from this experience I can add more demands for the Palestinians: the right of return, the right to dig our own water, the right to build houses . . . etc. Every Palestinian should have the right to drink coffee as much as they can without worries of having no bathrooms. And every Palestinian should have the right to pee every couple of hours . . . is that too much to ask for???

Ayah Bseisy

The Endless Tale

Freedom . . . Peace . . . Have become the first and last aspects in life to think and to care about, in a place and time completely free of them. I shall not forget that there is a replacement for them, like War! Now the scene looks so ironic. War, suffering, and tragic life, simultaneously, have become the only features that can be seen. Sadly, it is the reality over this place; freedom and peace are just our dreams that we strongly will to come true. It is a dream and ambition of one entity, and one nation . . . The Palestinians. We do not know what freedom is, or what it means by living in a secure place where your rights are fully preserved. Many successive generations had lived and died, many generations have been born, but nothing has changed since Al-Nakba "Catastrophe" in 1948 when Israel killed over thirteen thousand and displaced over 750,000 Palestinians. It is an ongoing process of exile, as an additional 400,000 persons were also displaced in 1967. We are the Palestinians who know the real pain, the real suffering, and the bitterness of life. It is not all about physical pain, rather pain of heart and soul. We resemble those who are being imprisoned for committing a crime. Those people were sentenced to be in jails for the rest of their lives. Far as I know, we do not deserve to be treated like murderers as long as we did not commit any crime. So, I guess the crime lies on the jailer—Israel. Unfortunately, the jailers are often not punished; consequently there is no one till now who could have stopped them. The reason stems from the painful reality; that they have power and authority but we do not. The more power you have, the more authority you have to control. But what happens when they are confronted by those who can, in a way or another, deter them? Here lies the disaster. Accordingly, they are targeting civilians.

Recently, Palestine is separated by the Apartheid Wall. They claimed it is needed for security, but the truth is that it has been done to block the Palestinians' movement. Those who have their homes close to this wall are not allowed to get out freely. They are controlled by small gates that are opened, by the soldiers, for a limited time. Children are held there for hours until they get to their schools. College students miss classes inevitably and professors are humiliated in front of their students. Elders are held on the checkpoints for a long period of time until they receive permission to get in and reach hospitals to get their treatment. Others have passed away on the checkpoints.

Israel is not only blocking our movement but also is restricting our daily consumption of water. The average daily amount per person in Palestine is 5 liters while it is 250 liters per person in Israel. This amount of 5 liters is barely enough for drinking and cooking. Are these really the only needs in life?! Israeli's simply do not know what mercy is. Merciless people are not humans but demons. It is also important to highlight the prisoners' issue. Thousands of Palestinians are held in jails without any reason and without it, men and women, adults and adolescents. Fathers were imprisoned fifteen, seventeen years ago or more, now their kids are students at universities. They have missed the chance to experience fatherhood. Let's also not forget those who died in prisons.

Israel calls us terrorists. It is undeniable that small Palestinian minority committed suicide attacks, killed Israeli civilians, but everything had been done as a consequence of their heinous crimes against Palestinians. Still it is very small number of Israelis who died in comparison to us. They have never stopped bloodshed since the beginning of Al-Intifada in 2000. They have never stopped demolishing our houses, and forcing displacement had never stopped but it is even increasing. We will never ever forget what happened to our brothers and sisters in Gaza strip. Israel had practiced a brutal military assault on Gaza Strip which resulted in the killing of over 1,400 and the injury of over 5,400 Palestinians. Their target was Hamas party, but Ohh! They missed their target and killed civilians—more than 355 children and 110 women. It was obvious that they were practicing collective punishment or what is called genocide. Soldiers were enjoying bombing whatever they see, and then a whole family or families were killed at once. Doubtless it is called "Massive War Crime". Over 11,135 building like "houses, schools, universities and mosques"in Gaza were damaged during that military operation. They became homeless until shelters were found for them. Israel trapped and terrorized people in Gaza and they are still saying "Palestinians are the terrorists"! It is not over yet. They are not satisfied yet, they want more. The Gaza Strip has turned into a "Closed Zone"; 1.5 million inhabitants are being detained. People are confined and isolated; they have been segregated geographically, economically, socially, and politically and deprived from basic rights and needs as a result of Israel's siege & blockade. Restrictions have been replaced on the movement of people to and from the Gaza Strip. Moreover, medical and humanitarian aids are not allowed to enter the strip. Much aid has been left in Egypt rotting and ruined. A lot of people died because they could not access proper medical care. Students who are studying in the West Bank were dropped back in Gaza and had not had the chance to continue their study. Israel prevents the movement of people on the pretext of pressuring Hamas, and that's the result. We shall not forget what happened recently with the "Freedom Flotilla" that was coming to Gaza carrying humanitarian aids. Israeli soldiers attacked the ship and killed up to 20 peace activists. They were not armed and nonviolent people only came to demonstrate peace and to bring the world's attention to the siege on Gaza. Yet we are the terrorists!

Israel occupied us and took over 3/4 of Palestine, including our capital, Jerusalem. They built their state and claimed ownership of our land as if it was one day written in their name. They believe that it is their promised land. They imposed on many to leave our homes, and now these Palestinians are refugees living in the Diaspora, who lost their identities, and still waiting for the right to return to their homeland. Israel continues to play its dirty games against the Palestinians in order to dominate. Building settlement is a continuing process; ongoing process of stealing our land, hence, separating farmers from their lands. Actually, settlers are not just residents in homes, but they have the authority to threaten and attack us. In my area where I live there is a place called "Osh Ghrab"; it is a public park which was built by our municipality. All of a sudden, settlers rushed into the place and threatened us with their guns to leave it quickly. Sadly, we have nothing to do!

Palestine's important location on the Mediterranean Sea and between the three continents (Asia, Europe, and Africa) makes it a valuable place for various economical projects. That's why Israel is opening their wide eyes on it. Israelis measures have made our lives so difficult. Taking the economic issue, living in a limited district leads to limited opportunities of work. The economic situation is getting worse and worse; the percentage of unemployment is increasing. Students are withdrawing from their colleges, and kids from their schools because their parents cannot afford paying the fees anymore. Instead, they search for work to help their families to stay alive. Israel had succeeded in employing their plan to increase the pressure on us to oblige us to leave Palestine. Consequently, millions of Palestinians had to leave the country and are spread all over the world. On the other hand, a great number of people have been tempted by a large sum of money to work in Israel. Guess what is the work? Building Israeli settlements!

All what we want is to stop this war, to stop this colonialism, and this humiliation, and to preserve our dignity, we just want peace. We have accepted the existence of two states on our land, and it's time for Israel to accept to end its colonial system and occupation of the Palestinians territories and accepts the rights of the Palestinians to be free. Immanuel Kant once said, 'a right violated in one part of the world is felt everywhere'. We are not denying the world's continuously unforgotten. endless efforts to provide humanitarian aid. However, what we need also from the world now is a little prayer for Israel to find their way to peace.

Peace on this World!
Katia Sa'ad

The Occupation

Palestinian people speak their suffering through the lines of this paper, as I am presenting Palestine's suffocated voice under the cage of occupation. We went through difficult as well as unforgettable moments because of their hatred for our beloved Palestine and its innocent inhabitants. They do not only carve terrible memories in our past, but they insist on demonstrating their daily existence in our present life through their creation of that high Separation Wall that surrounds our country. The occupation has had various harmful psychological impacts on our lives because of their cruel endeavors against the Palestinian people.

The Israeli occupation has had a negative impact on our collective psychology.

First of all, they humiliate us routinely on the checkpoints, as we are not allowed to pass unless we take off our shoes and all our metal accessories in order for them to be inspected by their machine. Thus, they intend to humiliate our dignity and make us feel inferior, so they can dominate us because they are aware that successful domination is not only achieved physically, but also psychologically. As a result, I experience, at the checkpoints, frustration and anger especially when I see young Israeli soldiers insult old people and oblige them to take off their shoes while they can't do so. Moreover, we need permission to pass the checkpoints and it's always given for a limited time. Thus, we are deprived of our freedom which is supposed to be one of the greatest rights for people, as we feel that we are caged in our country. Checkpoints complicate our lives, as they increase travel time and transportation expenses, so people, who can't afford it, may be deprived of visiting their relatives.

Second, they vent all their viciousness towards us by abusing mothers' emotions, as they beat their children in front of their eyes on the checkpoints with their brutal sticks, so they can see their tears and hear their scream. Thus, checkpoints are spaces of overt moral and physical violence. Then, they kill innocent people, making more widows and orphans. Thus, children are deprived of the care of fathers and women from the support of their husbands, as they must bear the burden of social costs. They destroy the structure of our families.

The shining sun faded and the black clouds overshadowed our beloved country, Palestine, in order to convert our smiley faces which are full of life and happiness to sad ones full of despair and crying eyes on every victimized martyr. Israeli soldiers invaded our country with their enormous tanks and bombs, as they were dispersed in every corner and house. They encircled the Nativity church and imposed a curfew, and they lifted it whenever they desired. We were living under suffocating stress, as all the local schools and universities were closed, so they aimed to produce an illiterate nation, so it would be easier for them to dominate us. Last night, while I was writing the lines of the events that took place during this invasion, I remembered the horrible events I experienced that morning.

It was six o'clock in the morning when I woke up fearful. My mother told me that the Israeli soldiers invaded our country; she added not to go near the windows because they were throwing bombs and shooting bullets. I felt depressed and ran quickly to my grandmother's house in order to hide in her room because it is much safer than our house. Then, all of us hid in her house to protect ourselves from any unexpected danger. Many of our Palestinian youth became innocent martyrs because they tried to defend their country from these invaders, but they couldn't because they didn't have effective fighting equipment. My mother used to bake bread in order to feed us because they lifted the curfew only once a week or sometimes every ten days. Although they lifted the curfew, they didn't let us go wherever we wanted; They lifted their guns towards my father's face while he was trying to help the nuns carry their stuff to their convent, so he was forced to go back in dread. I thanked God that he was safe. The forty days were gone, but our sorrowful memories are carved painfully in our hearts.

The occupation has now become a constant feature in our lives. But we have our Palestinian identity and heritage which will remain our treasure that no one can deny.

Ghada abu Kahlil

Palestinian Life in Jerusalem

Since the 1967 war between Israel and the Arabs, East Jerusalem has been occupied. The inhabitants of the city are Palestinians who are not allowed any kind nationality and are suffering from hard conditions, politically and economically, which have strained community life.

The Palestinian residents of the Holy City hold Israeli permanent residency and are allowed to participate in the Palestinian presidency and parliamentary elections. Israel does not recognize them as Israeli citizens and gives them travel document to use instead of passports. The education situation in the city is bad since many Palestinian children are not given a chance to study under fair and human conditions. Drugs, theft, and community problems are all part of the daily life of the Palestinian residents of the city.

Israeli policy is such that it views efforts to bring down crime as interference, and rejects any activity which the Palestinian Authority tries to order to fix problems which the Palestinians face in the city. Health, safety, community services, and education are all impacted. On the other side the Israeli security forces prevent any kind of leadership in the city. Any Palestinian that appears to be active as a leader is hunted by the Israeli security forces and threatened. The reason is that Israel is not interested in facing any kind of Palestinian leadership in the city.

While the Palestinians continue to suffer daily from economic difficulties, community problems, and a lack of any kind of freedom of speech or expression, the Israeli government continues to work in the field to change the picture of the Holy City and turn it into a Jewish city. The Israeli plan insists on turning the land to become completely Jewish and pressuring the Palestinians in order to make them leave the city. One example is the Israeli racist Separation Wall that resulted in separating Palestinian Jerusalemite families from each other. The Israeli law states that any Palestinian Jerusalemites who live outside the Separation Wall borders will lose their permanent residency and are forbidden from entering the city. This resulted in forcing thousands of Palestinians to live in small areas under bad circumstances.

It is important to mention that international law considers East Jerusalem under occupation and this means that Palestinian Jerusalemites should be treated as people under occupation, given their rights, and are assured human rights. Although Israel insists on considering itself a democratic and modern state it does not apply any of the above mentioned while talking about Palestinians. Instead it establishes special units to follow and hunts Palestinians so they will leave the city and surrender to Israeli pressure on them.

Ziad Abu Zayyad

A Wounded Life

My name is Moin Al-Atrash. I am now 25 years old, was born in the city of love and peace, the city of Bethlehem. I finished high school on the year 2002 and then went to study geography in Al-Quds Open University so that I would be able to be a geography school teacher, as while studying in the university I was also working in Bethlehem's Court, at the office of the citizens' public services.

On March 22nd, 2004, the Israeli occupation forces assassinated Sheikh Ahmad Yassin, who was physically disabled due to a full paralysis in my body and who was seated on a wheel chair. Many demonstrations took place in the cities of the West Bank and Gaza Strip to demonstrate the crime committed by the occupation forces against an old physically disabled man who doesn't move. There was a peaceful protest in Bethlehem city, as well as in the other cities, where school students, university students and others demonstrated peacefully to denounce this crime. When the Israeli forces started throwing tear gas and fired bullets against the demonstration I was among these protesters; the demonstration was full of school and university students who had nothing but their books. But I was wounded by a bullet that entered forcefully through my neck and exited my body from the back, causing me a complete paralysis. Disregarding my severe injury the Israeli forces prevented the ambulance from approaching toward me to give any medical help for over half an hour in which I lost lots of blood and later went into a coma. After allowing the ambulance to take me to the Governmental Hospital of Beit Jala, the doctors there decided to transfer me to Hadassah hospital due to my severe case and due to the poor medical possibilities in the Hospital. The soldiers tried to obstruct the ambulance from leaving to Hadassah hospital and they were searching the vehicle every time. But after a very long day, I finally arrived at the hospital where I underwent through the required medical surgeries, and after that the hospital issued me a report stating that due to my severe chronic injury I have paraplegia, "which means that half of my body won't be moving."

After two weeks, the Israeli army, with the cooperation of Hadassah hospital accused me of terrorism and expelled me from the hospital by transferring me back to Beit Jala Governmental Hospital. Then I was transferred to Jordan Hospital in the Hashemite Jordanian Kingdom where I stayed for a full month under intensive medical care & treatment because my health started relapsing and deteriorating in Beit Jala Governmental Hospital. After this the Jordanian hospital issued me a final report stating that there was no possible surgical interventions for my case, due to the injury and the cut in the spinal cord which caused me a permanent disability and that I need to be rehabilitated. After this report was given to me, I was transferred to The BASR (Bethlehem Arab Society for Rehabilitation). This all happened without my knowledge about the paraplegia because my family and doctors hid the truth from me due to the severity of my condition. When I reached BASR I insisted on knowing the reason why I was there and what's my case? To answer my questions a group of doctors and my family gathered and told me the bitter truth, the truth that I never wished to know! That moment I wished that they didn't acknowledge me about my situation. I felt like the world has closed its doors onto my face, everything was shut down and no one is there, I started crying, screaming, breaking things around me and hitting my legs to make them move. I couldn't afford to absorb the new reality. At that time I went into one of the worst psychological periods of my life, into a real psychological trauma. I started to think about how I used to walk on my legs and how I am now disabled and can't move, waiting for someone to help me after I used to offer help to people around me. I started asking every person: Am I paralyzed and disabled?

To tolerate and accept such a situation was very difficult and tough at the beginning, and this was one of the most difficult stages of my life, where I lost the ability to feel the lower parts of my body, to control the bowl, the bladder or any sexual functions. So I started wishing to die due to this very tough and difficult situation.

After a period of suffering, despair and lack of acceptance to the treatment, I didn't accept the idea of sitting on a wheel chair where all the doctors used to tie me up to the wheel chair with the help of the nurses to force me to get used to the wheel chair. And after this bitter and difficult time in my life passed a group of psychologists came and gave some intervention to me. They told me how necessary the treatment was in order to make my health better; they told me that I must sit on the wheel chair and that they'd be sending all my medical reports abroad and that in any minute I might be going abroad for the sake of treatment. But first of all I must accept the reality so that my health becomes better. After this I accepted to start getting my treatment and I was involved in the physiotherapy, occupational therapy and started sitting on the wheel chair until my health became better and I knew how to use the wheel chair very well.

Later after my health stabilized, the doctors came to me and told me that I would be leaving the hospital, and be going back to my home to continue my life. They also told me that my medical reports where sent to many hospitals but they didn't get any response from any of these hospitals. I was very disappointed by what I heard, and because I was going back to my home, I thought of what I might be doing while all of my brothers were at work but my mother was the only one there! So when I went back home, I used to stay for long hours on my bed, waiting for my brothers to help me sit on the wheel chair, and the hours used to pass as if it were a full year because of the nothingness I was living in while staying in my bed for so long. I started sleeping a lot, so much that I couldn't sleep at night times, so that made me take sleeping pills in order to sleep.

Until one day a person came to my home. This person was a social worker working at the YMCA. He told me that they teach the disabled some professions and make them small projects, so that they can depend on themselves and get out of the house atmosphere they're living in. I agreed to go with this social worker to the YMCA so that I would be able to go outside the house. So I spent there seven months where I learned how to carve the olive wood, but before learning the olive wood carving, I went into an intensive and long psychological therapy, to learn how I could deal with myself, how I could face the society, how to depend on my self and that what happened happened. I learned that there were other people like me and that there are many disabled people in the world who became creative, distinguished in their lives and became famous and important. I started thinking about how I could be like those people, so I started learning hard and quickly until I became a professional in carving the olive wood crafts and started curving the wood after designing its shapes using the computer. I realized that Bethlehem City is a touristic city, and the presence of the Nativity church might help me in marketing my small products or pieces like the crosses, and caves of Jesus, where I used to sell them to the eastern antiques shops that helped me to market my products. The specialists saw that I was capable of running a workshop and managing the marketing of its products where I used to bring all the work I used to do in the YMCA. The YMCA and the administration there realized that I was able to depend on myself and they built for me a small workshop. With the help of my family and friends I started working on carving the wood and marketing the products I carved around the city while the owners of the shops cooperated with me. I had an electric wheel chair where I would put my goods and go to the shops after introducing the people to me. Luckily the demand for my goods raised, so I started employing my disabled friends; where I wanted to turn this small place into a big workshop which would include a large number of the disabled people. I wanted to help all my friends to come out of the situation I already faced and overcome, and they all started working with me.

But my friends and I were all surprised that the Bethlehem market wasn't big enough to meet our needs, and that the occupation played a major role in that by building the wall and the sieges; the tourists stayed in Israel and only visited Bethlehem to pray. With that the occupation dominated tourism and helped spread the idea that the Palestinian people are terrorists. But my friends and I are still searching for outside markets abroad to sell our wood crafts around the world.

For my work I got the "Palestine International Award for Excellence and Creativity for People with Special Needs" in carving the olive wood, and I won $7000(U.S.). I used this gift to develop my workshop in which I had new and modern machines, but the market and the marketing of the goods were so weak.

My goal from learning to do these woodcrafts was to gather the heavenly religions and to continue the message of the love and peace, the message of the Prophet Muhammad and Jesus the Christ among my work by curving the wood, so I used to work for all religions and especially the Christian religion.

I am determined on sending the message of love and peace despite the paralysis caused by my injury. I am also determined that Palestine is to be the country of peace for centuries, and that it is a Holy Land that gathers all the religions, and the civilizations that have passed by Palestine. We are a nation who loves to live, and we love peace, but the occupation has killed the dove of peace. Also my problem is not with the Jewish people, for we live with Jews normally, but my problem is with the Zionist movement which wants to control us, occupy our country, control our resources and throw us outside of our country. There are Jews who love peace, and who stand by our side to defend us against the occupation's brutal acts.

We, the people of Palestine, love Peace, and we sacrifice so that Peace will prevail all over the world one day.

By Moin Al-Atrash

Um Salem and the Pillow

It was the year 1948 when the Israeli Arab war broke out. Suddenly, in the evening the Israeli troops broke into the houses of a village close to Um El-Fahem, which is a village north of Palestine and forced the people, through all severe means,—shooting, bombing etc. . .—to evacuate their houses. The people were helpless and were forced to run away in the middle of the night, leaving all their properties behind.

This story is about two neighboring families: Rushdi's and Salem's. Rushdi is a boy of five years, who was looking for his mother, the mother who was late to leave their house, as she was looking for her son too. Rushdi had to leave with his grandparents and was separated from his mother. The mother, who kept looking for her son could not follow, not knowing what happened to her son. Salem's mother hurried to take her baby, Salem, (6 months) who was fast asleep, but instead of carrying Salem she carried his pillow, leaving Salem in his cradle. She was out of her senses. When the mother took the pillow, the pillow whispered, "no, don't, please don't, I am not Salem, I'm his pillow, please go back! Salem is still in bed." But the mother wouldn't listen; she still carried the pillow instead and left the house! She hugged me—that was nice! But Salem was still there, what could I do? I tried to move from her arms so that she could feel I'm not Salem. But hopeless! And seeing Rushdi beside me, trying to draw his attention by pushing myself onto his shoulders—but that was in vain too. It was warm in her arms, I liked it! And I wished I was Salem".

Most of the village people left quickly, some of them carrying what ever they could take. They walked and walked for days until at last they reached a place near the city of Tulkarm. They stayed there for nights in the open, until some people came for help. They were the UNRWA who came with camps and set them up, and from that time we were called, "The Palestinian Refugees." Two or more families were squeezed in one camp. The two neighboring families chose to share the same camp.

"Now, said the pillow, "I'm in a good hands, with all my friends around me. But poor, Um Salem! When she discovered that she was carrying me—the pillow—and not Salem, she shouted and wept until at last she lost her strength, and fell asleep, with me on her lap. I couldn't help of course, I only gazed around to see the familiar faces like Rushdi and his grandparents. I could feel Rushdi's pain inside."

Rushdi was Um Salem's only companion; he lost his mother, but found love and sympathy with Um Salem. He always took care of Salem's mother, who got mad when she realized that Salem was left in bed. "Many a time, have children thrown me," explained the pillow. "Only Rushdi could come to my rescue and give me back to Um Salem, who in return used to hug me. Many a time have children mocked Um Salem, and kicked me a long way, but Rushdi used to bring me back and put me in her arms again. Sometimes he pretended to feed me, upon her request."

Rushdi grew up to be a patriot, and he always dreamed to hear any news about his mother. His grandparents always used to tell him stories of the past, how happy they were in their village which made Rushdi enthusiastic and yearn to see his home one day.

It happened one day, while Rushdi was listening to a program on Israeli radio, he heard a message of greeting saying: "From me to my son Rushdi, I send you my best regards, if you are still alive please inform me." You can imagine how happy she was, and how shocking it was for his grandparents—but how could he see his mother? Years passed, and Rushdi was always optimistic that he would once return to his village.

Twenty years passed, people were living miserably in camps. Rushdi's grandfather died, and he was left with his grandmother. Before his death his grandfather whispered in Rushdi's ear and said: "I have a treasure for you; it's hidden under the olive tree in front of our house at the village! Take care of it—it's yours."

And then in 1967 the Seven Day War broke out, another refugee problem arose. And a second occupation took place. More people were forcibly transferred from their land and took refuge in Jordan and other countries. For the first time people from the occupied land could come to what was called the West Bank. But Rushdi—would he be able to see his mother? Yes, it was a bright day, when a certain young man from his village, who made friends with Rushdi, came and took Rushdi to Um El-Fahem in his truck. It was forbidden for Palestinians of the West Bank to go there without permission, but Rushdi took the risk.

The friend dropped Rushdi in front of the house and I will leave it to the reader to imagine how touching was the scene. Rushdi hugged his mother!!

In the same illegal way Rushdi went back to his camp. There, the children shouted at him to tell him that Um Salem was very sick, and that she was in the street with the Pillow thrown around her. When she saw Rushdi, she said, "Salem, my son you are back!" But Rushdi handed her pillow and said, "Here's Salem." Um Salem smiled, put the pillow under her head, and passed away.

Rushdi was very sad; he sat at the doorway in contemplation. Then he hurried on foot—in spite of all the dangers—to the Olive Tree, dug the earth, and there was the treasure!! A Gun!!

But, what happened to Salem?? Did he die in his bed?? Has he been raised by some one who is kind hearted!! We don't know!

Lina Abed Rabbo

126

Unemployment

Every year thousands of Palestinian students graduate from different universities with different majors. It seems to be the most important moment in a student's life when they graduate, for now they can favor back to their parent, to get married, to make their dreams finally come true and become successful people. But that is not in Palestine because we have the scourge of wide spread unemployment and all dreams of youth are crushed by the Wall.

This is not strange in Palestine, as it's all crammed between the Wall, which is against the International Court in The Hague. Israel complains it's "protecting its citizens,"—protecting themselves from people who want to live. Gaza is a main example, where people are deprived of the simplest rights as human beings. Many students from ancient universities like Bethlehem University in Bethlehem, Birzeit University in Ramallah, Polytechnic In Hebron and Al-Azhar in Gaza and many others in Palestine, graduate with a gleam in their eyes for a successful life, but they are about to be crushed by the Wall, with the low job opportunities and wide-spread unemployment, in addition to the low wages in comparison to countries on the other side of the Wall (you can find a big different between Jerusalem and Bethlehem wages for example).

Imagine students giving up years of the hard studying, students who didn't hesitate any moment to get the highest grades and students who spent years of studying abroad to come home with high Bachelor degree, Master or even PhD, and find out that there are no jobs. Imagine the parents who didn't hesitate to give any help beginning with financial support and moral help so that they can see their children growing up into being men and women who can work and lead Palestine to the best. But the reality and the facts are much more painful and upsetting. Well, we do have precious strong working forces, but no places to work.

This reminds me of a friend who was a student in Al-Ahliye University in Jordan and after four years he graduated with an accounting major. I remember how his parents were proud of him and he told his dad: "now you can relax, I will work and support you." After four months of his hard searching he was employed as a waiter. I saw him with tears in his eyes and a small smile asking customers at the restaurant if they need anything else. I was in my second year at Bethlehem University when this happened; I felt so upset and angry when I saw him, so I told my dad that am going to withdraw from the university. Why am I supposed to study for four hard years? Is it because I want to get such an end? My dad told me: 'No, why so! we see the future in your eyes, you and your friends will determine the future of Palestine, don't get upset, cause it destroys Palestine, we are always optimistic because we are "The Sumud-steadfastness people"—we are called so because no one can defeat our determination and the will! They are trying hard to take us out of our land, and the only weapon left for us against occupation is education to make Palestine more powerful'.

However, we, the new graduates are the pillars of Palestine; we try to raise our country as much as we can from instructional, economic, political and even agricultural projects. As many successful companies and projects that have been created and grown, Israel is trying to beat us down by many ways, some by not allowing new technical machines to enter to our country or by delaying it, although you should know that some companies that were delayed by occupation have reduced unemployment among the Palestinian graduates. Also Israel is trying to beat us down by not allowing us to export our products to the other side of the Wall while our markets are full of the Israeli products that fiercely compete against the local product. You can see a wide range of products which are manufactured in Israel spread out in every Palestinian shop, but I'll bet you won't find any Palestinian products sold in any Israeli shop or market.

Another measure of economic repression is not allowing local products to be transported inside Palestine; many local products and also raw materials are forbidden to be imported to the West Bank from The Gaza Strip, even though there's a signed agreement in 2005 which states that about 400 trucks of exports are allowed to leave Gaza every day, but nothing leaves there! Imagine that the main raw materials, like iron and cement, which are very important to rebuild the destroyed and damaged factories and homes after the last barbaric war on Gaza are forbidden under the reason that Israel is afraid that they might fell into the hands of "Hamas." This caused many factories located in Gaza to be closed for good. The latest UNRWA statistics shows that nearly 3000 company and factory closed their doors and as an effect of that about 44% of the population in Gaza suffers from unemployment.

Another way is that Palestinian products are obliterated by Israeli companies; for example, recently they found in the south a famous olive oil that is known to be Palestinian best quality oil but it was fully obliterated and sold for a double price; when Palestinian experts checked this oil they discovered that it only have 20% of the Palestinian pure oil quality.

Otherwise Israel is trying to obliterate the Palestinians culture in many ways. All these ways are the main reason of the high unemployment percentage in Palestine, and for that I fully support the boycott of the Israeli settlement products campaign, for in this way we may give a chance to some of our local and successful products.

Now you see why I am right to hold full responsibility for unemployment to the segregation Wall. It's because we are not allowed to move into Israel, so that laborers can work there the way they used to do before, and if they were able to get a permit to go behind the Wall they have to stay on the checkpoint from the early mornings at around 4am to cross it and go to work at around 8-9. People can't go to the other Palestinian cities for they'll be wasting many hours on crossing checkpoints, and that is terrible, and exhausting. There are not enough organizations where the people can work in as well and that's another reason. Also we can't forget the confiscation of the agricultural lands, which stops the people from working on them.

So briefly these are a few reasons of why the unemployment rates are high in Palestine; it is not because we're not educated or because we are lazy but because of the poor investment environment due to the occupation, the financial sieges imposed on the Palestinian authority and the endless practices by the Israeli occupation.

Palestine, as all countries around the world, aims for peace, freedom, justice and to have a good economic situation among the other strong countries. But occupation is not giving us any chance. We don't have an airport, we can't move in between the West Bank cities so that we can work in the NGO's or the companies around Palestine! So how are we supposed to fight unemployment? We have a powerful workforce but sorrowfully it is crammed inside the walls. *UNRWA* spokesman *Christopher Jones* said: 'Gaza folks love manufacturing and entrepreneurship, give them a chance and they will earn their living.' And I believe in that because all we need is a chance, only one chance to show that we can build a better world, because we are smart, educated and a good hearted people who are willing to live in total peace accompanied with justice, full human rights and freedom.

By Jiries Mriebeh

A Letter to the American people: When abnormality Becomes Normal!

Dear People of the United States of America,

I was so excited when I was asked by a friend of mine to write about Palestine and Palestinians in this book directed to you, free Americans living in America, Country of freedom. It's just an excellent chance to address such a distinguished people about an ongoing occupation of 62 years in modern history.

My 6 months stay in the States between 2005 and 2006 was one of my life's unforgettable experiences. There I knew how much the people of the States are lacking the truth that is shown in media about the Israeli-Palestinian conflict. And there I was so eager to tell my story and explain to the people there the situation I was living in.

Today, let's talk about the wall that Israel started its construction around the Palestinian occupied territories in 2003. A wall that is controversial about everything, including the naming. While the Israelis call it in Hebrew "separation fence" and "security fence" or "anti-terrorist fence", Palestinians most commonly refer to the barrier in Arabic as racial segregation wall, and some opponents of the barrier refer to it in English as the "Apartheid Wall." The International Court of Justice, in its advisory opinion on the barrier, wrote it had chosen to use the term "wall."

Upon completion, this "Wall" will be 472 miles long, twice the length of the 1949 Armistice Line (Green Line) between the

West Bank and Israel, with varied heights from 8 to 12 meters. It will annex 46% of the West Bank locating approximately 385,000 settlers in 80 settlements between the Wall and the Green Line. All the Palestinians need a special permit to go to Israel through the Wall, including all those Palestinians who live between the Wall and the Green Line, which means that they need permits to be on their lands and in their homes. Actually this kind of dilemma was lived by me when I had to do the visa interview in Consulate General of the U.S. in Jerusalem. Then, and with a friend of mine and after we were not given the permits for Jerusalem, we had to pass the wall "illegally" through a gap in the Wall made by Palestinian workers who work in Israel.

In 2006, I had the same problem applying for my visa before going to Italy to do my Master's degree there but then that gap in the Wall was closed. So I had to meet with a friend of mine who lives in Jerusalem on the checkpoint to give him my documents to take them to the Italian Consulate.

In the states I knew and experienced the meaning of living and traveling with freedom. I'll never forget the time I traveled from Washington, DC to North Carolina by car. The Wall, during that trip, made it to my mind and I started thinking about life there and its difficulties, connecting them to the reasons for the high rates of immigration that Palestinians suffer from, to scenes of those pregnant women in ambulances waiting for a permission to pass a checkpoint to go to deliver, and finally thinking about the wall that prevented me and still prevents many others to go to Jerusalem, 6 miles from Bethlehem, to visit family, work or just participating in a mass in the Holy Sepulcher Church.

There in the States and after this unforgettable trip I knew how much I was mistaken, together with most of the Palestinians, thinking that the situation we're living in is normal. Yes, the Palestinians think it is normal having a Wall, checkpoints and curfews that limit their movements, maybe because they were raised and lived under occupation and unfortunately they need to travel abroad to see and understand the abnormality of their lives.

Finally here's a simple innocent question for all of you, world's greatest powers who want to see an end to the Israeli-Palestinian conflict, such as the United States:

Is it easier to transfer all the Palestinians abroad to show them how it is to live in freedom, than it is to put some pressure on Israel to work for peace and end the occupation?

Thank you so much for your time and hope to see you soon in a free Palestine.

Sincerely yours,

Issa Sakhleh
Bethlehem
6/28/10

Why is the World So Crazy About My Hair?

Some here, some there

Ask me to take of my "hejab"

Why is the world so crazy about my hair?

Is it black, blond, or gray

I said I will not say

Guess what guess what

You have to guess—no answer from me

In a world that doesn't excuse me

Not showing you my hair or my body

But wanting you to feel a heart, mind, thoughts, and the human in me

In this "cool" world civilized I can't be

Even holding in my hand a PHD

Unless the other hand is holding a glass of beer

With a gun to my head you said be free be free

I say dig more dig more

Dig a little deep

To fly with my soul that has always been free

I'm not the image you see on TV

I'm a strong Palestinian women wearing "hejab"

Take a look at your self and stop judging me.

Ayat Omran

Why, Why, and Why?

Have you ever felt distinguished according to a colored plastic thing?? Have you ever felt worth nothing and with no given nationality on your documents??Well it is what we feel when we look at our ID cards which actually give us more difficulty than anyone else can imagine. It's simply a piece of paper covered in a plastic thing with different colors than other areas in Palestine yet this means we are different. We have no nationality on it, nor do we get any other privileges of a Palestinian or an Israeli.

As a child, you never even try to think of such stuff as the ID or occupation or checkpoints, but as for me it was our daily life even if we never acknowledged it until later on. I never even thought of what I would encounter and go through. We only went in our own car and never used the buses except for close by areas that were 10 minutes away. Even when we went to areas like Bethlehem or Ramallah it would be in our car sometime in the afternoon. When we went back home, it would be dark at night so that I would fall asleep in the car only to wake up again when we have reached our house. It was only when I went to one of those far areas in the bus that I knew how it was like to pass a checkpoint.

It was about 7 years ago; I was still going to school, when my mom and I decided to go for a day out. We took the bus and went. We reached Ramallah, went shopping and had a day out where we ate laughed and had a really good time. But it all changed on our way back. I always heard of the term, "checkpoint," yet I had never encountered any one without being with my parents in a car; also without having my own ID card. It was the first time I saw a really long queue of people waiting to pass what was no more than a five minute walk while the sun burned their skin. Standing there made me think: why is that we have to stand in line to pass to our houses? Are we considered such a huge threat? I could not understand what was going on or, to be exact, why we had to go through such trouble to reach the places in our country.

After that day I really hated going from one area to another and I only would go to places around Jerusalem to have fun. But after three years it was time for college. I actually wanted to study abroad but as I was the oldest daughter in the family, it was hard for me to do so. So I applied to universities around Palestine and got accepted at Bethlehem University. Now my daily checkpoint-adventure was renewed and it had to be something usual for me; except even now it isn't.

Knowing that I had two older cousins living in the same building as I did was a relief for me because I would go and come back with them in a private car as I always had done when I went to areas that required passing a checkpoint. So the first year went smoothly. But, after my cousins graduated, all the trouble I had avoided approached. On the first day of the second year I rode in the bus and went on my way to the university with my friends. We were all double checked for our ID's and university ID's as well to make sure we weren't missing anything. But on the way back there the story of our daily trouble began. The bus was loaded with all kinds of people: old, young, children, tired people, people in a hurry, and people who seemed to have all the time in the world to spend. We were listening to music so we didn't care much for the people in the bus until it was time to get checked. Going down from the bus, knowing it must be over 95 degrees outside since we were at the end of August, my old questions re-emerged. Why is that it's us and only us that have to go through this? And why is that its only we who have to get our bags, vegetables, clothes, accessories, and IDs checked before being able to pass to reach our work, houses, and families?

After a long half an hour of being checked, bags being thrown out because, according to those who are responsible at the checkpoints, food is not allowed to pass from one area to the other in the same country!, with people half tired, half angry wanting to go home in any possible given way, and being humiliated for carrying a bag of sweets or because your child is carrying a harmless toy with him that according to the soldiers is something worth having to wait and get humiliated for, you get a chance to pass by on your way and yet—even then you don't know what will be waiting on the way for you.

But no, we were not able to pass back to the bus that day. My friends and I were laughing at a joke one of them made and we did not care that we were on a checkpoint and that we had to stay quiet since we were acting as we usually do when we go anywhere. That was when the soldier actually did not like what we were doing. We never got what he was trying to do or why he would not want to see us laugh. But we did not care and we laughed even more. I guess that was when we really got on his nerves. He was really furious but we didn't know it was because of us or because of something that happened earlier but that only made us really angry. Like why should we not be allowed to pass back to the bus because we were laughing? Or why was it that because we laughed he got angry? Is it actually forbidden for us to laugh? Aren't we humans the same as they are? Anyway, we asked what was going on, and why was this happening, and the soldier simply said, don't laugh and you'll pass back to the bus. I got furious and I asked him if he heard a joke wouldn't he laugh? Actually after a while of arguing we found out he thought we were laughing at him and that's why he stopped us. I guess he never had enough self esteem to know that he wasn't a clown for us to laugh at.

So as you see this is only a simple example of what goes on daily. Actually it is worth nothing next to what people who do not have the blue ID face. My friends who live in the West Bank and have a West Bank ID cards face a whole lot worse on checkpoints and sometimes, even with permits, are not allowed to pass the checkpoint for a lot of reasons. One of my friends wanted to come to Jerusalem once since it was the Easter and she wanted to buy stuff and hang out. First she got into the bus at one of the checkpoints and as they said people with permits cannot pass from here she had to go back and try her luck at another checkpoint. Yet on the other checkpoint she had to wait more than 2 hours arguing with the soldiers before they would allow her to pass and at the end she returned home because all the time that was left for her after all that was one hour and she was so upset that she could not have fun.

All this is what a person faces daily at checkpoints. Students with student ID cards that are shown to soldiers get humiliated and sometimes even made fun of for going in buses, studying in universities, or for any other reason they find. Young people who are under 16 years old and are not issued an ID card yet, get humiliated even more, as some soldiers tend to mock them and ask them about their ID's and start talking to them and telling them, "no, you are lying. You are over 16 you are married and you don't carry your ID because you want to illegally pass from one side to the other" and that they are to get down from the bus and are left waiting for hours on the checkpoint while the soldiers are laughing at them, and they cannot even find the words to defend themselves. Even more, at a daily checkpoint you could see old people get humiliated from young soldiers where they jumble with all their sacks and tend to mess up their stuff and they even make fun of them when they start asking what is this and what is that and stupid questions that everyone knows that they know what they are.

All this is the daily life a normal Palestinian leads, going to work and passing by one or more checkpoints on the way to and from their work, school, or university, being humiliated by small things or huge things daily. It's not easy, yet that does not mean we will ever lose our faith, for we all dream of having a magic wand to change all that we desire to change, but what we all do not know is that we all actually have that magic wand and it is called the will. It is the will to go on and move on to higher places and make things better for our future and the generations to come. Yet, we still ask so many questions that we never find a satisfying answer for. Why is that it is us and only us that have to lead such a daily process? And why is that we are the ones that are considered without nationality, yet in our hearts we belong to a place we call WATAN "homeland"? Why and why and why . . .

Wala' Dakkak

What it is Like to be Living Here

Throughout my life I have been put in many situations where foreign people would take minutes to comprehend that I was Palestinian. What is it that is so shocking about me being a Palestinian? It is about stereotyping. I hate, where they think we are not supposed to be educated or good looking. People think we haven't got the simplest appliances; they get really shocked if I speak English well or even French. They are most likely to doubt that I am either lying or that I am from Bethlehem, Pennsylvania, USA. Believe me, it does not feel good at all being me through these moments. However, I like it, I just love to prove to the world that we are not who you think we are, we are made of thoughts and opinions as good as if not better than yours.

I know our life in Bethlehem is far from perfect, I am trapped, I feel like a mouse that just got used to the maze. Bethlehem looks like a huge prison, and it makes me furious each time I don't get a permit to cross the checkpoints. I can't visit my sister's house in Jerusalem, I can't go on a two day trip, I can't reach Haifa or Nazareth with the church youth group and I can no longer go to the old city of Jerusalem and visit my grandmother as I used to when I was little.

I know we live in a somehow terrible situation, politically, socially and economically. However, I think I have made the best out of my life. I am an honor student in Bethlehem University, I am socially active to the furthest extent, I am a member in youth groups, I take the responsibility for summer activities in the local church community center, I take courses outside the domain of my studies and I do give my big family a lot of attention.

As for me, I have big dreams, I am planning on continuing my higher studies and doing something in life because I want people to remember me when I die; I don't want to be another number that passed on this earth.

I feel proud to be Palestinian, I actually feel special. Despite everything we have passed through, I still feel special, optimistic and great.

I have high expectations for my future, and I am not planning on letting my self down.

Grace Awwad

To Jerusalem

Dear Jerusalem:

You are the sun of my rainy days . . . You are the reason of my existence . . .

Living in your neighborhoods gives me a special feeling of tranquility . . . hearing the echoes of your mosques and churches' sounds bless my days . . . I decided to write to you, my mother, to express my love and to tell you about my daily life . . . when people ask me what does it mean to be a Jerusalemite? I stay silent for a moment then I begin telling my long chain of stories of endless suffering . . .

Being a Jerusalemite means to pass through the check points everyday . . . Being a Jerusalemite means to endure all the kinds of humiliation that Israeli soldiers cause just because of loving YOU . . . Being a Jerusalemite means trying hard to endure the pain when you watch the scene of your ancestors' house tarnished by a Zionist family . . . Being a Jerusalemite means to love Jerusalem more than anything in your life . . . Being a Jerusalemite means to have the stamina to steadfast in your land and to water it from your own blood . . . Its soil will be part of your flesh . . . Its trees will be your children . . . Being a Jerusalemite means to carry the image of the golden dome in your mind to light it with its vital shines . . .

Beloved Jerusalem I promise to love you and to keep you in my heart and mind . . . you are a bit of heaven . . . long live Jerusalem . . .

Shurouq Ayyad

www.ingramcontent.com/pod-product-compliance
Lightning Source LLC
Chambersburg PA
CBHW061308280526
45784CB00002B/936